The Foreclosure Phenomenon™

How to defend your home from an impending foreclosure

by

Joaquin F. Benitez

to my good friend Celito

from J Benitez

TELEMACHUS PRESS

THE FORECLOSURE PHENOMENON™

Cover art and design by Ranilo Cabo

Published by Telemachus Press, LLC
http://www.telemachuspress.com

The Forclosure Phenomenon™ is a registered trademark of Joaquin F. Benitez

Visit the author website:
www.theforeclosurephenomenon.com

ISBN: 978-1-939337-21-4 (eBook)
ISBN: 978-1-939337-22-1 (Paperback)

Version 2013.03.18

Printed in the United States of America

10 9 8 7 6 5 4 3 2 1

Contents

The Foreclosure Phenomenon™

How to defend your home from
an impending foreclosure

Foreword

The Foreclosure Phenomenon™ is your survival guide to learning everything you need to know about foreclosures, the struggles you are facing, and the proper steps you need to take so you can "learn how to defend your home from an impending foreclosure." In this book you will find everything you need to help you defend your home from foreclosure situations.

Written with firsthand knowledge of the foreclosure process we join the author as we walk the long journey he took over twenty years ago. His personal experience through the foreclosure process has enabled us to find the right help and advice at a time when we need it the most to survive this financial pandemic. He has learned from the experience, recovered his financial losses, and wrote this book to help others going through similar situations.

Foreclosure is a major challenge that lies ahead of thousands of families across the United States and Canada. It is spreading like wildfire in North America, causing financial chaos at all levels in our society. We may not even realize the full financial impact this phenomenon has had on us and will continue to have on us for many years to come. Whether it affects us directly or indirectly, at some level, we are all affected by it.

In a bold move the author created "The Foreclosure Phenomenon" to help you formulate strategies, to come up with ideas and gather information about this overwhelming process for foreclosures so that you can understand the rules of the game. If you are experiencing financial challenges remember six words that helped him reach his financial goals **"Everything is going to be o.k."**

The author wants you to understand the commitment that it will take to save your home. He wants you to realize that you are not alone. He gives you his experience and firsthand knowledge to help you reach your dream of saving your home, not only for yourself but for your family as well.

It was not only an honor but a privilege to share some of the author's story in the hope of knowing that through his difficult times he was inspired to write this book in the hope of helping others.

Raymond Aaron
New York Times Bestselling Author
www.UltimateAuthorBootcamp.com

Testimonials

Joaquin's perspective on foreclosures is fresh, new and exciting. He offers an array of strategies and methods any homeowner can easily implement to successfully save their home from foreclosure. I would encourage every struggling homeowner to read this book!

Raymond Aaron

New York Times Bestselling Author

www.UltimateAuthorBootcamp.com

Joaquin's perspective and advice is outstanding. This easily implementable information is long overdue and much needed in today's economy. Any homeowner, who is struggling financially, needs to make this book their foreclosure defense road map. I recommend this book to every homeowner who has encountered financial challenges.

Shawn Shewchuk

Bestselling author of Change Your Mind, Change Your Results

www.changeyourresults.com

Joaquin provides an easy process to learn how to handle a foreclosure with an added personal touch. An honest and heartfelt approach guides the reader to take charge of their situation, by providing strategies to help slow down the foreclosure process. This book is easy to understand and follow. I encourage every struggling homeowner to grab a copy of this book!

Dr. Vijay Nielsen, D.M.S., H.D.

Acknowledgments

I am so fortunate to have so many people in my life to thank. The following list is far from complete. I would like to thank my family for their support and words of encouragement as I struggled to put on to paper one of the most unpleasant periods in my life. Those words of encouragement motivated me to offer these words of reassurance and hope to others.

To my wife Alicia, who always encourages me and pushes me to be the best person I can be. To Blanca Alicia, my oldest daughter who in spite of being busy raising her three little children, has spent countless hours helping me put this book together. To Cristina, Marcia, David and Andre for their encouraging words. They have no idea how much I valued their positive comments after reading the original manuscript.

But most importantly, I would like to thank you, the reader. If you have ever wondered whether you mean anything to an author, you do! This book was written with you in mind and I will be forever indebted to you. THANK YOU!

Introduction

The first reported case where the term *foreclosure* was used occurred in 1728 and over the last few centuries properties have continued to go into foreclosure. This procedure has now become a widespread occurrence and has a common process within our court system. In recent years it has ballooned into what we now know as the *Foreclosure Phenomenon* and has spread rampantly over the United States and Canada like wildfire, bringing along with it financial ruin and catapulting our economy into a state of disarray. Thousands of families have been affected by it. We may not even realize the full financial impact that this phenomenon has had on us and will continue to have on us for many years to come. Whether it affects us directly or indirectly, at some level, we are all affected by it.

When we find ourselves in a foreclosure type of situation, it gives us a sense of helplessness and despair with no end in sight.

It is a terrible feeling isn't it? Right now every phone call, every letter, and everyone that approaches your door all seem to be threatening or demanding money from you. The bank is threatening to take away your home, your car is being threatened with repossession, and someone else is threatening to seize your bank accounts and all of your life savings. Not only do you not know who to turn to for help, but also, you don't know what your rights are. To make matters worse you don't know what the bank collection agent can do to you!

I have personally experienced the emotional stress and psychological pressure of a foreclosure situation. My personal financial difficulties go back almost twenty years. Since then, I have recovered from my financial losses, I have learned from that experience, and I am now writing this book to offer help and advice to those who find themselves entangled in an impending foreclosure proceeding.

Here is my first instruction, and I want you to write this down and look at it as often as you need to during this whole process. Are you ready?

Everything is going to be o.k. Close your eyes, take a deep breath and say, "**Everything is going to be o.k.**"

I know it may seem easy for me to say now that I have overcome my financial difficulties. I will admit that it is easier to say it than to believe it, but remember you need to keep a level head if you are going to survive this ordeal. These six simple words have a special meaning to me. They are the very same words my wife used to say to me when we were in the midst of our own foreclosure nightmare. She used to say those six simple words to comfort me, to encourage me, to give me hope at a time when I had none. It was at a time in my life when I was at my lowest emotional state, with no hope in sight. Please engrave these six simple words in your mind and, regardless of the outcome, remember: **Everything is going to be o.k.**

There are quite a few things that you can do, but first we have to take an inventory and figure out exactly where we are in the process. In addition, you cannot do and must NOT do two things:

Panic and do NOTHING.

We sometimes make the mistake of thinking that 'to do nothing' is to postpone a decision, when in actuality 'to do nothing' is to make a choice by default.

"When you make a choice, you change the future."
—Deepak Chopra

You literally cannot afford to make the same mistake that thousands of people have already made. The consequence of doing nothing affects not only your finances but also your physical, emotional, and spiritual well-being. The truth is that your situation will not improve and it will not go away on its own. The worst thing that you can possibly do is to ignore your problem. The bank can and will repossess your home if you do not take the appropriate actions.

By doing nothing, you are in fact choosing to lose your home. If you are reading this book, you must realize that you have a choice to make and that the choice is yours alone; no one else can do it for you. For whatever reason, you are experiencing financial challenges and have fallen behind on your mortgage payments. The last thing you need is your mortgage broker threatening to begin a foreclosure proceeding against your property, undoubtedly seizing most, if not all, of your life savings in the process. You may pose the question, "Is there something, *anything* that I can do to stop the bank from taking away my home?"

The answer is an unequivocal **yes**. While every person's financial situation is specific to them and the challenges they face are unique, there is usually something that can be done. In some cases, the problem can be addressed by simply generating the funds to make up the missed payments and administration fees. Other cases are more complicated and will require some serious thought and consideration.

The objective of this book is to give you enough information to encourage you to make the decision to take a stand and confidently defend your home against this phenomenon. By creating a strong defense strategy and developing a thorough battle plan, you will be able to rescue your home from foreclosure and endure as little financial and psychological damage as possible, regardless of the outcome. We will cover not only the technical proceedings necessary to derail an impending foreclosure proceeding, but we will also deal with the traumatic emotional issues that come because of it. You could save your home!

Remember, take a deep breath, and say to yourself, **Everything is going to be o.k.**

Chapter 1
The Foreclosure Phenomenon™

OVER THE LAST few years, the term **foreclosure** has become a common word in North America. Foreclosure events are constantly being mentioned on the news and in our day-to-day conversations. You can see its devastating effects everywhere you look. Many people are worried and maybe even scared about the possibility of losing their home. Even though the word foreclosure has become a common word in our everyday vocabulary, many people have misconceptions about what a foreclosure is and what it means. Most people have the thought that a foreclosure happens when the 'rich bank' takes away a poor persons home. If you go out to the street and survey one hundred people and ask for their definition of the word foreclosure, the majority would probably struggle to give you a clear and definite answer.

Although foreclosure is an extremely broad topic, I will provide a simplified explanation. *When a real estate property is purchased, the buyer must borrow money from a moneylender to make the purchase.* Unless you've been hoarding cash under your mattress, you will need to go to a moneylender to borrow the money needed to complete the real estate purchase. *The homebuyer enters a contract with the moneylender and one of the terms specified in the contract is that the moneylender has the right to take possession of the property and sell it if the borrower fails to make the mortgage payments as agreed upon in the contract.*

Foreclosure is the only legal proceeding by which the moneylender can terminate the borrower's interest in the property after the borrower has failed to make the mortgage payments as specified under the mortgage contract or agreement. Once the moneylender takes possession of the property, they will try to sell it in order to recover their money. However, in some jurisdictions in Canada there are different provisions where a creditor can take steps to sell the debtor's home without going into a foreclosure proceeding but pursuant to a judgment issued by the court.

Why is foreclosure a phenomenon?

The *phenomenon* I speak of refers to the ferocity and speed by which foreclosures have been occurring in recent years, and continue to occur at an alarming rate. It is spreading like wild fire in North America, causing financial chaos at all levels in our society.

RealtyTrac (reported by CNBC) published a report in November of 2010 and found that in October 2010 there were 332,172 foreclosure filings, a four percent drop from the previous month. That is 332,172 newly foreclosed properties in a single month. They also reported that the rate of foreclosed units had not changed since October 2009. At the writing of this book in the summer of 2012, RealtyTrac reported that in the month of July 2012 there were 191,925 new foreclosed properties. One must admit that the foreclosed numbers in July 2012 look much better in comparison to the numbers reported in 2010. However, if you consider the number of properties that have been lost to foreclosure on a monthly basis over the last five years, you will realize that the numbers are staggering. Even the improved numbers reported in July 2012 are disproportionately high.

The financial losses caused by this phenomenon have reached into the trillions of dollars, creating havoc for financial institutions. In fact, the damage caused by this phenomenon has been so great that many top banking institutions have ceased to exist, due to the unprecedented number of foreclosures. The situation has become so devastating that governments have had to intervene financially by pumping billions of dollars into the banking industry to rescue not only major national banking institutions, but also the whole world's financial system.

The purpose of this book is not to dissect the reasons for which this unprecedented phenomenon has taken place. The purpose of this book is to offer help and sound advice to those who are in danger of falling victim to this phenomenon by presenting information, ideas, and strategies that can be quickly implemented to save one's home from the financial pandemic that is afflicting our society.

How does this phenomenon affect you?

The sad reality is that this phenomenon is like a plague. It has no respect for anyone at any level of our social and economic structure. It does not only affect you as an individual homeowner, but affects top executives in financial institutions to homemakers struggling to make their mortgage payments.

This phenomenon has far-reaching consequences. It is not just limited to banks and homeowners, businesses and investment firms; it even impairs the way that local or municipal governments operate. It hinders the government's ability to provide its citizens with adequate basic services. At the writing of this book in the summer of 2012, there was a news report in which three large cities in the USA had filed for bankruptcy protection because of this phenomenon. One of these cities is San Bernardino, California and I anticipate there will be many more cities that will follow suit as we feel the full impact of this phenomenon. We are all being affected in one way or another.

To illustrate how local governments are affected, consider this scenario. As a homeowner facing foreclosure, the last thing on your mind is paying your property taxes. Local or municipal governments generate the majority of their revenue from the collection of property taxes. This revenue constitutes a large portion of their operating budget. If the local government is unable to collect the property taxes from your property, they, in turn, will not have the money to function as a government. Their operating budget will be thrown out the window and they will not have the capacity to provide basic services for their citizens. Additionally, they will struggle to complete their payroll and therefore they will need to take drastic and painful measures to reduce costs. Some of the cost cutting measures may include the reduction of their labor force by offering early retirement and/or layoffs. The financial condition of many local governments is critical and some of them are near bankruptcy.

Consider this, if a handful of people fail to pay their property taxes, it is not an issue for a local government. However, when hundreds, if not thousands, of homeowners are losing their properties to foreclosure and as a consequence fail to pay their property taxes, local governments have a *big* problem. They will not have the funds to function as a government and provide adequate basic services to its citizens. Services such as, law enforcement, firefighting and emergency medical services will all be affected. If they do not have the funds to provide basic services, you can only imagine what will happen to infrastructure maintenance and repairs. I am not making this up; it is the reality that we are currently living. This phenomenon creates a sense of insecurity and fear in everyone and with good reason. Can you see the implications and the effects of this phenomenon? Massive layoffs are occurring, even reaching local government levels (such as in San Bernardino, California). You need to realize that things are not looking good. Layoffs at this level create even more pressure on the banking system because, when homeowners are let go from their places of employment, they experience even more challenges in meeting their financial obligations—potentially producing another wave of more foreclosures.

We started to feel the effects of this phenomenon towards the end of 2007, many economists and financial experts argue that the worst of this phenomenon is behind us. My personal opinion is that the worst is yet to come and when it comes, it is going to hit us with such force and speed that we will not know what has happened. The reason why I have the boldness to say this is that the U.S. federal government has done nothing to correct the current problem. Their decision to inject massive amounts of cash into a troubled system has not fixed the problem; it has only relieved the financial pain for a short time. In reality, the government's decision has made the situation worse. At some point in time, someone must pay back all the money that has been borrowed and with interest. I feel that the time to pay back all this money is soon approaching and if you are not prepared for the real financial tsunami that is imminent, you will suffer much financial pain.

I am not an economist and I am not claiming to be an expert on financial matters. However, common sense will tell you that you do not get out of debt by attaining more debt, especially when you do not have the means to pay for your existing debt. As an example, you do not get out of credit card debt, by getting another credit card with a higher credit limit. Especially when you do not have a secure source of income that allows you to pay down your original debt.

If your income is not sufficient to cover all your monthly expenses and you are forced to use your credit card to make up the difference, you are in a deficit position. Getting more credit will never solve your long-term problem. At some point in time, you will have to pay back all that money you borrowed with interest and since you are in a deficit position you will not be able to generate the money to pay it back. Continuing with this credit card example: Once the lender or the credit card company refuses to give you more credit, or refuses to increase your credit limit because they begin to consider the possibility that you may not be able to pay them back, at some point the creditors will demand their money back. You are given only two choices, one is to take a dramatic cut in your operating budget (as we have seen in some European countries as of late) and the other is to declare bankruptcy.

Sadly, this is exactly what the U.S. Federal Government has done. They have borrowed money that is beyond their ability to pay back. I have no idea how all of this will end, I just know that it will not be pleasant.

You may argue that since you live in Canada you may be immune to the U.S. financial problem. Since the U.S. is Canada's major trading partner, and the world's largest consumer, whatever happens in the U.S. impacts not only the Canadian economy, but the global economy, as well.

As stated previously, the purpose of this book is not to correct the financial crises or eliminate the foreclosure phenomenon. My hope is that by giving you a brief overview and some basic knowledge of how our financial system works, you will be better equipped to defend yourself in a foreclosure proceeding.

We have already covered the catastrophic effects of this phenomenon and the dire condition of our current financial situation. In the following chapters, we will cover how to prepare yourself mentally and emotionally to face the challenge of defending your home in a fore-closure situation. By the time you finish reading this book, you will have received enough information to mount a strong defense. However, the outcome will depend on your ability to follow the given instructions and, more importantly, the desire to defend your home.

Chapter 2
The Bank's Worst Kept Secret

PERHAPS YOU WILL be shocked to find out the bank's worst kept secret, or perhaps it is something that you already know, or maybe it was something you knew but it never dawned on you as a valuable piece of information that could be used to your advantage. However, before we go there, it may be beneficial for you to obtain a better understanding of what foreclosure is and the legal procedure that the bank must go through to take possession of your property.

Foreclosure definition and procedure

Foreclosure is a legal action that a moneylender (such as a bank, credit union, and/or private lender) can take if a person who borrowed money (through a mortgage or deed of trust), stops making payments on their loan or mortgage. Foreclosure law allows the moneylender to take possession and subsequently dispose of the person's property in order to recover the money lent to the borrower. However, the lending institution must first obtain permission from the court in the form of a court order in order to proceed. There are two key words here, one is *mortgage*, and the other is *permission*.

A *mortgage* is a contract or an agreement set out between a homebuyer and a moneylender. The homebuyer commits to repay the loan on a monthly installment basis until the full amount plus interest is paid in full. The moneylender requires security for the loan. The homebuyer pledges the property as security or collateral for the loan. In the unforeseen event that the homebuyer fails to make his or her regular monthly payments as specified in the mortgage contract, the moneylender can exercise the right under the law to take possession of the property and dispose of it in order to recover the original loan amount plus fees and penalties.

Lending institutions protect themselves by securing the loan with the property that they are financing. The pledged security (the real estate property) gives the moneylender some assurance that the property owner will pay back the borrowed money on time as specified in the mortgage contract agreement.

According to a recent U.S. census, roughly 70 percent of all properties in North America have a mortgage. That means that 30 percent of North Americans who own a property are not at risk of losing their home and will not be directly affected by this phenomenon. The 30 percent of fortunate homeowners that own their homes free and clear will still be affected indirectly. Due to the large volume of properties in foreclosure, their property value will drop significantly to be in line with the current real estate market value. They are not in danger of losing their homes; however, they will have a difficult time selling their property, if they choose to do so. This indirect impact has everything to do with supply and demand. At the present time, there is a large supply of properties on the market and a very small pool of buyers.

The other word that is of importance when outlining the definition of foreclosure is *permission*, court permission to be exact. What this means is that for a moneylender to exercise his or her right to foreclose and dispose of your property due to non-compliance with the terms of the mortgage contract, the moneylender must go to court to obtain permission and obtain a court order to take away your home. The moneylender must follow a specific procedure stipulated by law to obtain that court order.

What this means is that you will not lose your property automatically for missing a couple of mortgage payments. The moneylender does not have the legal right to start a foreclosure proceeding until after you have stopped making your mortgage payment for at least two to three months.

An advantage that you have with the pre-established court proceeding is that you can predict with complete certainty what the moneylenders next step will be. There is a specific procedure that the moneylender must follow and legally comply with. It can take several months for this legal procedure to go through the court system. This allows you to prepare to counteract the actions of the moneylender in his pursuit to expropriate your property. The foreclosure procedure and length of time to process varies from state to state in the United States and from province to province in Canada, depending on the location of the property and the laws governing that state or province. Therefore, obtaining legal advice is strongly recommended.

Below is a brief overview of how the moneylender will start the legal foreclosure procedure. Once you have missed your first mortgage payment, the moneylender will ask you to make up the missed payment. If that strategy fails to produce any results, then they will start demanding immediate payment and threaten to start a foreclosure proceeding. If the threatening phone calls fail to produce results, the moneylender will exercise his right under the law to recover his money by starting the foreclosure procedure. Normally, the moneylender will first send you (the registered homeowner) a letter demanding payment, typically called a "**Notice of Default**." If you fail to comply with the repayment demand, the moneylender will take his first legal step, using the court system, to recover his money. The moneylender will then start to foreclose on your property by filing a complaint against you, the registered homeowner, with the court for *noncompliance*. The complaint that the moneylender will file is called a "**Petition to Foreclose**." In some cases they will launch a lawsuit[1] against you at the same time. This petition stands as the lender's notice to you, the homeowner, that they are officially and legally asking the court's assistance to recover the money that they loaned to you.

If you have missed a couple of mortgage payments and you have already received the letter of "**Petition to Foreclose**," the very first thing that you must do is to **seek legal advice**. A real estate legal advisor will be able to inform you on how to best respond to this letter, how much time you have, to whom you must respond and other specific information regarding foreclosure laws governing your state or province. Perhaps you may be saying to yourself, "I can't afford to get legal advice." The truth is that you cannot afford *not* to get legal advice. It is extremely important that you get legal advice as soon as you possibly can. Since the real estate laws vary in every state and/or province (if you live in Canada) and you need to know how to protect yourself within the court system, you must gain knowledge of your rights and obligations specified under the law as a homeowner.

Furthermore, you need to take part in the court proceedings. If you fail to respond to the letter of "**Petition to Foreclose**" within the allotted time (in most cases it is 21 days) after receiving the letter (or 'being served' as it is also known), you will forfeit your rights as a homeowner and will be unable to defend yourself in a court of law.

---

[1] Additional information on lawsuits is available in Chapter 6.

The foreclosure process will continue without you. Therefore, you will lose your right to defend your interest in the property.

If you have already received the letter of **"Petition to Foreclose"** and you have not filed a response, I strongly suggest that you do so immediately after obtaining legal advice. In the **"Petition to Foreclose"** letter you will find the date by which you must file a response, and additional details of where and to whom you are required to send your response.

I would like to emphasize that you must submit your response by the specified date. If you decide to send your response by mail, you need to account for a few days delay in delivering your response. Please do not wait until the very last day to send it by mail as it will arrive late and you will forfeit your rights as a homeowner. Once you have filed your response in the allotted time and have directed it to the appropriate addressee the first major step has been taken. Now, no one can take any further steps against your property in regards to the foreclosure procedure without notifying you.

After you have filed the **"Response to the Petition to Foreclose"** letter, there is not much more you can do except wait to for another court document called a **"Notice of Hearing,"** which tells you when you must appear before the court to hear your case. During the court appearance, the lending institutions legal representative will request permission from the court to foreclose on your property immediately due to lack of payment, and they will have all the evidence to prove their case. During this first court appearance, the judge in most cases will only give the lending institution an **"Order of Nisi."** An **"Order of Nisi"** is a conditional order granted by the court where the homeowner is given specific requirements they must complete by a specific date. However, if you fail to appear at the court hearing, the judge may determine at that time that you are not interested in defending your interest in the property and the order to foreclose may be granted if there is no one there to challenge the decision. This is the most important reason for you to file **"Response to the Petition to Foreclose"** and appear at the court hearing.

The **"Order of Nisi"** indicates that a decision to your case has not yet been reached. This indicates that the final judgment or decision will be settled on a future date, unless it has been invalidated by certain specified contingencies. These contingencies could mean that you as the homeowner have arranged to repay the bank all of the late payments, penalties, and court filing fees. This could be done by successfully selling your property or at the very least showing the court that there is a strong possibility that you can arrange alternate financing for the property. It is during this time that you can present your case to the judge, and explain the reasons that have caused you to fall behind on your mortgage payments. During this time you are also able to prove to the judge that you are a responsible person fallen on hard times and that you are doing something to resolve the situation. The judge will give you time to fulfill your obligations with the bank and to compensate the lending institutions for their losses. In this case, the judge will set another court hearing in a month or two to see if you have made any progress with your financial situation. As long as you can prove to the judge that you are making progress to repay the bank, the judge will not grant the lending institution an execution order to repossess your home.

Another beneficial reason to attend the second court hearing is to ask the judge for as much time as possible to get your finances in order, to obtain alternative finances, or to secure additional funds to pay off the mortgage by selling your house. The judge will want to know the basis for the extension request—what further steps you have taken to resolve the situation? As long as you are making significant progress, the judge will grant you additional time. This allotted time is sometimes referred to as the *redemption period* in which the judge is giving you time to redeem your property in order to fulfill your mortgage agreement with the bank.

If the *redemption period* ends, and you have failed to prove to the court that you are making significant progress towards compensating the lending institution, the court will have no choice but to give the moneylender a final **"Order to Foreclose."** At this time, the judge will give you a date by which you must vacate the property, and if you fail to vacate the property voluntarily on the specified date, a bailiff will come to your house and remove you from the premises, by force if necessary.

Once the redemption period is over, the moneylender will ask the court for the right to have their real estate agent list your house for sale. If the court grants the moneylender the right to sell your house, the moneylender will obtain an order called a **"Conduct of Sale."** Once the bank receives this order, you can no longer sell the property. This stands as the final notice informing you that you have lost your home.

This is a very short description of the process involved in a foreclosure, and in these few pages you have learned a lot more than most people will ever know about a foreclosure proceeding. Unfortunately, most people who have lost their home didn't know most, if any, of this information. They never bothered to become informed of their rights. Due to this lack of information, they failed to take any action, which could have saved them a great deal of stress.

Now I would like to impress you with a secret that is not really a secret. It is common knowledge, yet many people don't know it; and because they don't know it, they fall victim to the foreclosure phenomenon.

The bank secret

The bank does not want to take away your home! I know it sounds absurd, but by the time you finish reading this chapter you will be persuaded that it is an accurate statement. The very same people, who have been threatening you with foreclosing on your property since you fell behind on your mortgage payments, don't really want to foreclose on your property.

Allow me to go a step further: The very *last* thing that the bank wants to do is foreclose on your property. It is an extra expense that they don't need to incur and it will cost them thousands of dollars to take a property through the foreclosure process. Now you may be asking yourself: If that's true, then why are they threatening me with foreclosing on my property? What do they really want?

There is a simple answer; the bank collection agent wants to scare you into making up the late mortgage payments, and by doing so, ensure you will continue to make your mortgage payments on a regular basis until the end of the term as specified in the mortgage agreement. The threat of foreclosure is the only legal tool that the bank has at their disposal to recover their losses.

Furthermore, once the bank initiates the foreclosure process, the banking laws regulating the banking industry require the bank to report that property as a non-performing asset. Doing this will hinder the banks capacity to borrow more money and it does affect their overall credit rating. The bank must try to avoid having to report a non-performing asset on their books at all cost. In many cases, banks intentionally delay initiating a foreclosure proceeding for up to six months, and even a full year, to avoid reporting the property as a non-performing asset.

The *'non-performing asset'* problem or the NPA as it is commonly known in the banking and financial industry, affects the banks in more ways than you and I may care to know or understand. These three simple letters strike terror in the banking sector and business circle today. The dreaded NPA rule simply states that: When interest on a loan or any other monies is due to a bank and it remains unpaid for more than 90 days, the entire bank loan automatically becomes a non-performing asset. The recovery of a 'loan gone bad' has always been a problem for banks and financial institutions. They will go to great lengths to avoid having to report a property as a non-performing asset.

Why would three simple letters "NPA" cause such terror to a financial institution? What are the consequences of having to report it? There are a number of problems that will arise from having too many NPAs on the (bank) books. I will list a few so that you have an idea as to why the bank really does not want to foreclose on your property.

- The bank owners (shareholders) will not receive a market return on their invested capital and in a worst-case scenario, if the bank fails, the bank owners and/or shareholders will lose most, if not all, of their invested money.

- The bank depositors will not receive a market return on their savings and investments and in a worst-case scenario, if the bank fails, the depositors will lose the uninsurable balance on their money.

- The bank will redistribute the losses to other borrowers by charging higher lending interest rates on car loans, mortgages, and credit cards, which will hamper their ability to grant new loans because their lending rates are no longer competitive with the rest of the industry.

Furthermore, the bank must have a certain amount of dollars in cash reserves. If their levels of non-performing assets become too high, they will have to put more cash into their reserve account to compensate for these non-performing assets. This means they now have less money to lend, which means they have less money they can make. In addition, they now have to deal with a house that they don't want because it will become a money pit. Furthermore, they will not be able to make a profit on it because of the way mortgages are structured.

Banks, in their quest to maximize their profits, structure mortgages in a way that they are paid the majority of the interest up front or at the beginning of the loan term. This is called a frontloaded mortgage and all mortgages are structured in the same way. This means that in the early years of your mortgage you have not built much equity in the house because the majority of your mortgage payment was slotted to pay for the interest on the loan. If you have been making mortgage payments for less than ten years you have not built much equity on your house, especially now with the recent housing valuation bubble.

Many times banks find that their asset (your house) is worth less than what they lent out on it based on the current real estate market. Once the bank takes ownership of your property, they not only have an administrative and legal nightmare, but they are about to take a financial bath!

Even though I am not a bank advocate, I am certain that if you were in the bank's situation, you would be forced to do the exact same thing. The bank does not have any other recourse. The only legal recourse available to them is foreclosure in order to try to minimize some of their losses.

Suppose that you had to borrow money to start a business, and for the sake of comparison, let's suppose that your business is losing money every month. How long will you be able to keep the doors of your business open? If you don't sell the business quickly or find someone to take it from you at a discount, eventually your entire investment will be wiped out. At some point in time, you must make the decision to cut your losses and figure out a way to pay back your lender after you have disposed of your business.

Banks face this situation every month. They must cut their losses to preserve their very existence. Many large U.S. banks, such as Washington Mutual, ceased to exist for this very reason. In some cities in the U.S. like Las Vegas, Miami, and Phoenix, there are hundreds of properties going into foreclosure every month. So much so that in many cities, the court system, which handles foreclosure cases, cannot keep up with the massive amount of properties being foreclosed and, furthermore, it is poorly equipped to handle the tidal wave of bad home loans.

Am I asking you to be sympathetic to the bank collection agent, especially the one that is causing you so much grief? No, I just want to explain the lender's financial situation and obligations so that you have a broader view. By having a wider perspective and a deeper understanding of the situation, you will appreciate its point of view and understand its needs. Knowing this very relevant piece of information will empower you to present the lender with intelligent alternatives to solve its problem and yours, since you now know that lenders don't want to foreclose on your property; and you don't want them to foreclose on you. You now have common ground to work out an agreement that will satisfy both of your needs.

Can you see the predicament that lending institutions find themselves in? On the one hand, they are losing money by not receiving your mortgage payment and on the other hand, they can't really afford to foreclose on you because of the negative consequences that this will bring them.

One of my former instructors in a contractual law course made the following observation: "If you owe the bank three hundred thousand dollars and you can't pay them back, you have a problem. If you owe the bank three hundred million dollars and you can't pay, the bank has a problem." It is apparent that many banks, including the big name banks, are facing challenges related to property foreclosures. World leaders in the banking industry, such as the Washington Mutual bank (worth an estimated $307 billion dollars in assets), Continental Illinois National Bank and Trust (worth an estimated $40 billion dollars), and IndyMac (worth an estimated $32.01 billion in assets) have failed in the financial crisis. These extremely wealthy and seemingly stable banks have gone under due to their inability to meet their financial obligations.

Financial institutions are in the business of selling money. To put it in clear and simple terms, this is how the financial institutions operate:

- Banks borrow money from the federal bank and depositors at a low interest rate.

- They sell this same money to people like you and me at a higher rate.

- They also borrow money from you and me at an extremely low interest rate through *guaranteed security of deposits* which are locked in for one, three or five year terms.

- They take this money and sell the *same* money back to you at a significantly higher interest rate through secured and unsecured loans.

Secured loans are those that are collateralized by a physical object like a car, boat, or a house that the bank can take back if you fail to make the payments. Banks usually charge a lower interest rate for secured loans compared with high risk unsecured loans like credit cards. The bank's profit is generated by the spread created between the interest rate that they pay you on your money and the interest rates that they charge on the money that they lend out. The bank pockets the difference.

While this is an admittedly simplified explanation of how financial institutions operate, the bottom line is that banks are in the *"money buying and selling business."* It is unprofitable for a bank to have a vault full of money that it is unable to lend out to others. The bank pays interest on this money to the Federal Bank and to its depositors. Therefore, it is in their best interest to lend this money out to a willing loan recipient. For the bank to make any money, it must loan out the funds in its possession, or find some sort of investment vehicle that will guarantee a rate of return greater than its cost of borrowing.

Banks always try to minimize their exposure to potential losses and they have specific written procedures that loan officers must follow to guard the bank from unforeseen eventualities. For this reason, the bank requires collateral, something you value, and that you will not be willing to walk away from easily. The bank wants to have some assurance that you will make regular monthly payments on your loan. If you do not make the regular monthly payments, the bank will start to repossess whatever item was pledged as a security for the loan.

Consider the main motivating factor for a bank to be in business. It is not to provide a service to the general public; they are in business to make money. In a foreclosure case, they will most likely lose money. Now you need to consider the bank's motivating factor for stopping its monetary losses. As the old saying goes, "the best way to make money is to stop losing money." Therefore, when you approach the bank to find a workable solution, you will be taking the position of a business partner that is willing to help them minimize their losses. Whenever you approach someone and you offer him or her help, they will be willing to sit down with you and listen to what you have to offer.

While you may not realize it, having this simplified knowledge of how banks operate is very important. Once you understand how a bank operates, and the motivation of the mortgage broker, you will gain the confidence to call the bank and discuss a solution to your situation where both parties can come out as winners. This knowledge will empower you to go to your bank with boldness and negotiate a repayment plan for the missed payments. It may even allow you the ability to renegotiate the mortgage and obtain either a lower interest rate, or at least a monthly payment that you can afford. You will talk to your banker or loan officer on the same level and with confidence. You will not approach them as a beggar seeking mercy. You will be able to engage the lending officer as a businessman ready to work out a fair deal for both parties.

Having the knowledge of how lending institutions operate and their two main motivations (which are to make money and to stop losing money) will allow you to develop some degree of confidence when arranging to speak with them. Can you see a shimmer of light at the end of the tunnel?

Chapter 3
Gathering Information

IN THIS CHAPTER, we are going to cover specific ways to acquire all the relevant information that you will need in order to defend your home. This is one of the biggest obstacles you must overcome. The biggest challenge for you will be to find reliable sources of information. Most likely, you have no idea what information is required, and worse yet, you do not know where to find any of it. In addition, due to privacy laws, no institution will release private financial information to anyone except you. This step is something that no one else can do for you—you must take action.

If you have read this far, I am going to make the assumption that you are experiencing financial challenges and that you have already defaulted on your mortgage payment or payments. If this is the case, you most likely have found yourself being harassed by a bank collection agent and you must be receiving threatening phone calls at home or at work (if you are currently employed). I am quite certain that by now, every letter that comes in the mail, every time the phone rings, and every time someone knocks on your door, your heart stops for a second or two. You expect the worst. You believe that every stranger that approaches you is going to demand a payment of some kind. Furthermore, you are angry, upset, and scared. You do not know what to do and worse yet, you don't know what the bank can do to you.

In addition, you must be receiving a lot of mail from your creditors demanding immediate payment, something that you are not capable of doing. Some of these letters may be coming from the bank that holds your mortgage. Once you start receiving threatening letters from the bank and other creditors, you instantly become afraid. Your thinking becomes erratic. It feels as though there is no end in sight.

Unfortunately, we react to the situation in the most natural way humans do when in a state of panic. We hide! We shut ourselves in from the outside world as a way of protecting ourselves. You may even stop answering phone calls or avoid people all together, especially family and friends, the very same people that may be able to help you. Instead of seeking help, we shut ourselves in—the exact opposite of what you should be doing.

At some point in time, you may even become so discouraged or frustrated that you simply stop opening the mail or start throwing the unopened mail in the garbage. As a warning, it may be prudent to reconsider that practice. You are about to receive an official letter from the bank that holds your mortgage demanding official immediate payment. This is a very important letter, because it is the kick-off for the foreclosure procedure. This letter is called **"Petition to Foreclose,"** as mentioned in Chapter 2. This letter is the instrument that the bank uses to officially inform you that they have made a petition to the court to grant them an order to take back the property that was pledged as collateral for the loan. This means that the bank is legally making a motion to repossess your home.

Obtaining legal advice

The very first thing that I would suggest you do is **obtain legal advice**. If you live in Canada, you will need to seek advice from a foreclosure specialist or a litigation lawyer. As mentioned earlier in the book, it is extremely important for you to obtain legal advice to learn where *you* are in the foreclosure process and what your next steps should be, as foreclosure laws vary from state to state and from province to province if you are in Canada. You will need to consult a real estate lawyer to explain how the foreclosure procedure works in the state or province where your property is located. In addition, you need to find out what your rights and obligations are under the law.

Another reason for consulting a real estate lawyer or a foreclosure specialist is to determine how much time you have available to prepare a defense and to find out what will be the bank's next legal step.

If you can't afford to hire a legal advisor or a real estate lawyer, call your local legal aid office and ask for assistance. I can't emphasize enough the importance of obtaining legal counsel. Any action that you take without legal advice could make matters worse for you. When you speak with your real estate lawyer, or legal advisor, you must have copies of all the original mortgage documents and all of the letters that you have received from your lending institution. After reviewing these documents, your real estate lawyer should be able to tell you where you are in the process.

At this point the real estate lawyer should be able to advise you on what steps you must take or, at the very least, inform you of the next step the bank will take to expropriate you from your property.

The information you need to gather from the real estate lawyer is as follows:

- Where you are in the foreclosure process

- How much time you have to prepare a defense

- An overall idea of how the foreclosure laws work in the area where your property is located.

From that point forward, it will be up to you to determine if you need to hire a real estate lawyer to represent you in court.

The mortgage payoff balance

Your current mortgage balance and the mortgage payoff balance could be two completely different numbers and in many cases, these two figures could be thousands of dollars apart.

Your *current mortgage balance* is the amount that appears on your mortgage statement at the end of the year. The *mortgage payoff balance* is the amount of money that you would have to pay the bank if you were to pay your mortgage in full today. The mortgage payoff *balance* includes your mortgage balance, late payments, interest on late payments, late fees, legal fees, filing fees, closing fees and prepayment penalties.

Prepayment penalties are something that most people fail to consider. I mention this because in many mortgage contracts, buried in the small print, there is a clause called 'prepayment penalties' and it outlines how the prepayment penalty is calculated. This clause states that you can pay your mortgage in full at any time during the life of the loan. However, by choosing to do so, you will be required to compensate the bank by paying a penalty equal to three months interest on the balance of the mortgage or an interest differential payment penalty, whichever is greater. That means that if the interest differential payment penalty is greater than the three months penalty, they will charge you whatever figure is greater. In many cases, the penalty amount turns out to be thousands of dollars. If this hidden clause is part of your mortgage agreement (I call it hidden because no one tells you about it until you want to sell your house) it could cost you several thousand dollars in penalties that will be added to your payoff amount. Needless to say, it is very important for you to find out what the total payoff figure is.

This information will be of great value if you conclude that finding alternate financing with a different banking institution is the best path forward. In addition, should you conclude that selling your property is the best solution, you need to know how much money you will end up with, once you pay off your mortgage in full, plus realtor fees. Not knowing what the real payoff figure is will cause you to end up with a lot less than what you anticipated. Furthermore, you could end up in a deficit position with the bank and at closing still owe the bank money apart from the original mortgage amount.

The easiest way to obtain this information is by calling your bank. On your bank statement there should be a phone number where you can direct all your inquiries. When you call them, ask them for the current mortgage balance and the payoff balance. Simply ask them this, "If I were to sell my home at the end of the month, what would be the payoff amount, including all fees and penalties." They should be able to give you that information over the phone. However, you want this information in writing, as it could become evidence later on in the process. Ask the customer service representative to send you a letter stating the mortgage balance and payoff balance that they quoted you over the phone.

The current value of your property

The real current market value of your property is a very important piece of information. This is the starting point—everything hinges on this information; therefore, you need this number to be as close as possible to the current real market value of your property. This number will be of upmost importance when you start to brainstorm your options and will be useful as a negotiating tool when you speak with your mortgage collection agent.

How is the value of a property determined? The answer is that there is no real science to determining the exact value of a property. We can estimate the value of a property, plus or minus a few thousand dollars. However, the real value of a property is determined by how much a person is willing to pay for it. In other words, the real value of your property is not determined by how much you think it is worth or how much your neighbor sold his house for six months ago. The real value of your house is the amount of money that someone is willing to pay for it today.

There are two ways to obtain this information; the first one is to hire a real estate market appraiser. The market appraiser will charge between $200.00 to $300.00 for their professional (guessing) services and in the majority of cases, their estimates are on the low end of the scale. As mentioned earlier, their estimate is only their personal opinion of what the value of the property is and they don't want to be sued later on, either by you or by the bank for evaluating the property for more than it is worth. If you sell your house for more than the estimate, then you will be happy and there will be no need for a lawsuit. However, if they give you a high number and you end up selling your property for much less than the estimate, you will most likely try to sue them. Needless to say, I don't have much confidence in their evaluation.

The second way of obtaining more accurate information on the real value of your property is through your local real estate broker. However, to obtain accurate numbers you will need to spend a little more time analyzing the information and doing some simple calculations.

Start by calling one of your local real estate brokers, perhaps someone that you know, or someone that has been referred to you by a family member or a friend. If you don't know anyone, just grab the yellow pages or Google a real estate agent in your area.

I would like to stress that you will need to obtain good and accurate information from the real estate agent. To successfully complete this task you may have to call several agents until you find one that is willing to work with you. Another word of advice when choosing a real estate agent, do not choose one that just obtained his real estate license. Choose someone that has been around the block a few times, so to speak. Work with someone that has at least ten years of experience. You need a knowledgeable person with experience who is able to give you a good/true estimate on your property based on his or her understanding of the current market conditions and acquired knowledge over the years in the business.

Real estate agents and brokers are like everyone else who provides a service; they want to be paid, and if they do not sell a property, they do not receive any income. I mention this because you need to be careful about how you approach the agent and the information you share. If you tell the agent that you are about to lose your house to a foreclosure, he may be less willing to help you, because in his eyes he will be wasting time. It may not be in your best interest to volunteer this information during your first call.

When calling the real estate agent or broker, you might say something like, "I am considering putting my house on the market, but before I take that step, I would like to have a good idea as to what my house is worth in the current market." By approaching it in such a way, you are simply making a factually accurate statement. You need to know the value of your house to be able to consider if it is feasible to list your home in the current housing market.

Any real estate agent will be happy to hear that you want to list your house with them. Because if they have many listings, they are more likely to close on a deal that will earn them a commission.

Continue with the conversation and set up an appointment. Ask him to come to your house for an evaluation of your property. At this point you may want to make it clear to them that you are not ready to list your property yet. All you want to do at this time is gather information about the current value of your property. Be clear that you will be making the decision to list your property sometime in the future—once you have analyzed all the facts and are able to conclude that the best decision for you will be to sell your property.

Be warned that when the real estate agent comes to your house to evaluate your property, they will aggressively try to get you to sign a listing contract. You must be polite but firm and tell them that at this time you are only gathering information, that if you make the decision to sell your house, it will be done after you analyze all the facts. Furthermore, tell them that, at this point, you are only interested in finding the real market value of the property to use as a point reference for your calculations.

Another fact to consider is that many real estate agents are struggling financially. They are desperate for money and, in many cases, they will try to list your property for less than the real market value of the property. The main reason for doing so is because, if the property is listed for less than the market value, they will potentially be able to sell your property quicker and receive a commission sooner than if they list your property at full market value. Therefore, once they give you an evaluation, you should ask them to prove their estimate numbers.

If the agent refuses to give you any information until you sign the listing agreement or obtain some type of commitment from you, simply call someone else. Your biggest challenge will be to find someone that is willing to give you the information that you need.

This is the information that you require:

1. Fair market value of your property. Once the real estate agent walks through your house, ask the agent for his/her professional opinion as to what would be the fair market value of your property. After you get a response, ask the following question, "If I were to put my house on the market today, what would be the listing price in order to get it sold in the next 30 days?"

2. Confirm the market value of your property. You do this by asking the broker to provide you with a list of comparable homes similar to yours in square footage, style and upgrades. Ask for the **sold comparables**, not the listed comparables, in your area over the last six months to a year. **Appendix A: Part A** contains a

sample spreadsheet titled *"House Sale Comparables"* you can use to collect this information. If you would prefer a free downloadable copy, please visit us at:

http://www.theforeclosurephenomenon.com.

The list of sold comparables that the broker is going to provide you will have one house that was sold at a very high price and another one that sold at a very low price, discard the properties with the highest and lowest numbers and work with the ones in between. What you are trying to obtain is the average sold price per square foot in your area. If you require assistance figuring out how to calculate the average, refer to **Appendix A: Part B** for a sample spreadsheet titled, *"Market Value Comparables"* or visit:

http://www.theforeclosurephenomenon.com
for a free downloadable copy.

Now that you have figured out the average sold price per square foot in your area, you can determine how much your house is really worth under the current market conditions. Now a little side note: Even though your house is worth the fair market value, you may have difficulties selling it because there may be one hundred other properties in your neighborhood for sale competing with yours.

3. Ask the real estate broker how many properties in your neighborhood are currently on the market?

4. One last question: How many days, on average, is a property on the market before it is sold?

Personal financial information

Thus far we have been focusing on gathering the information related to your property. However, you will also be required to find the cause of your problem and that has everything to do with your *personal financial information*. It is obvious that you are experiencing some financial challenges since you are not able to make your mortgage payments and there could be a number of reasons for it. Regardless of the reasons, the fact remains the same. You have fallen behind on your mortgage payments and you need to do something about it.

Have you ever taken the time to do an income and expense sheet? In one column you list all of the household income that comes in every month—your total income. In a second column, you will list all of your expenses. In the expense column, include all expenses such as minimum credit card payments, car payments, food expenses, car insurance, health insurance premiums, utility bills etc. You need to list every payment you make. You need to account for every dollar that comes in and goes out of your house.

Many times, when you have this list in front of you, you may realize that there are some unnecessary expenses that you are able to eliminate and some other expenses that you could drastically reduce. By so doing, you are freeing some money that could be used somewhere else. Often this simple exercise will cause you to see things from a different perspective and make you realize that by making some minor changes to your lifestyle, your financial situation can change so much that your financial problem solves itself.

In other cases, you will find that your budget is so tight that you are operating on the bare minimum. However, you will have a real number on how much of a deficit you have every month. This simple exercise will give you a real picture of your financial situation[2].

This information becomes very important when you enter into negotiations with the bank collection agent. You will be able to show him your monthly income and expenses, how much of a deficit you have per month and how much of a mortgage payment you can afford. This is a very significant piece of information that can be easily verified by the bank. By doing so they will be able to either work out a repayment plan for your late payments or lower your mortgage payments to help you keep your house.

Information summary

You should obtain the following information from a legal advisor:

1. How does the foreclosure process work in your area?

2. Where are you in the foreclosure process?

3. How much time do you have left to sell your house or to make alternate financial arrangements?

From the bank customer service representative:

4. What is your mortgage balance?

5. What is your mortgage payoff balance?

From the real estate broker:

---

[2] See Appendix B for a sample income and expense sheet or to obtain a free downloadable copy, visit us at www.theforeclosurephenomenon.com

6. The current market value of your property.

7. The number of properties listed in your area.

8. How long it will take you to sell your home.

Your personal financial information:

9. Income and expense sheet.

10. A list of creditors and the minimum payments owed.

What do you do with this information? Now we are going to analyze all the facts and begin to create strategies on how to best approach and solve this problem. Assuming that you have gathered all the required information, how do you feel so far? Do you feel empowered? Just by having all the facts in front of you removes much of the confusion that has been crowding your mind and has negatively affected your emotions. The simple step of gathering all the facts will bring clarity to your thoughts and comfort to your heart. Perhaps now you are beginning to understand the facts and are encouraged to know that there may be a way out of this stressful situation!

Let's move on to analyze the information and start to think of ways to defend your house against the foreclosure proceeding. Regardless of the outcome, remember, **Everything is going to be o.k.**

Chapter 4
Analyze the Gathered Information

I WOULD IMAGINE that before you had this information, you were scared and confused because you simply did not have all the facts in front of you. All you knew was that you were late on your payments and that the bank could come at any moment to take away your home. Now you know more than the bank collection agent and that will give you the upper hand in the negotiation process.

Now that you have started to sort through all of the gathered information, you will discover the reality of your situation. By simply analyzing the information, you may discover that your particular situation is not that bad. As mentioned many times in the previous chapters, it is extremely important that you gather accurate information as it will set the proper strategy in motion for your particular situation. Whatever decisions you make will be based on this information and if the information is not accurate, it will cause you to use the wrong strategy, thereby producing undesirable results.

By quickly comparing the payoff mortgage amount and the current market value of your property, you can easily find out the severity of your situation. You could be in one of the following three situations:

you could be *ahead, breaking even,* or *upside down* (also referred to as underwater).

Let us look at each one of situations individually and find out what it means and what strategy you could use to solve the problem.

You are ahead, what does it mean?

You are ahead if the total payoff amount on your mortgage is lower than the current market value of your property. By simply comparing the two numbers, you may be happily surprised to find out that your property is worth more than what you owe to the bank.

Wow, what a nice surprise! Suddenly, the insurmountable problem that you thought you had dissolved before your very eyes. Simply by you doing your due diligence in finding the facts, you have solved your problem. Well, not quite, we still have to deal with the foreclosure proceeding. However, if your property is in foreclosure, being ahead is the best situation you can find yourself in.

A recent study conducted by mortgage and real estate data firm CoreLogic published an article at the end of September 2011. Their study concluded that in the U.S.A., all properties with a mortgage 48.5 percent, had at least 25 percent positive equity in them. This report also found that only 70 percent of all the properties have mortgages, the other 30 percent of the properties are owned free and clear.

Before you get too excited, I would like to point out that the study was conducted on a national level and that 25 percent positive equity is a national average. In some states like Nevada or Arizona, the average will most likely be much lower than the reported 25 percent national average. This percentage will vary in different regions of the country due to the large number of foreclosed properties in those areas. Other parts of the country, like the New England states, will do better than the 25 percent positive equity national average.

Nevertheless, it means that if you have a mortgage on your property you have almost a 50 percent chance of being in a better financial position than you thought you were. It means that you have nearly a 50 percent chance of walking away from a foreclosure proceeding with money in your pocket and with little or no damage to your credit record, if you choose to sell or refinance your house.

If you are ahead, you are by far in a better position than those who find themselves in the other two situations. You have a number of options available to you. The quickest solution may be to get a home equity line of credit, refinance your property with another financial institution, or sell your property. Any of these options will solve your financial problem. In the next chapter, we will cover this in greater detail, specifically covering how to determine what your best option is.

You could be breaking even, what does it mean?

It simply means that the mortgage payoff balance is the same as the current fair market value of your property. According to the same report listed above, it was reported that 29 percent of properties with mortgages fall under this category.

If you are facing foreclosure and your property falls under this condition, your situation is not that bad; there is something that can be done. Your options however are somewhat more limited than someone who is *ahead*. There are at least two different strategies that can be used to improve your situation to come out of a foreclosure with little damage to your credit record and perhaps with some cash in your pocket. It will depend on your ability to negotiate and on the flexibility of your lending officer. We will cover the strategies to deal with this situation in the next chapter.

You could be upside down or underwater, what does it mean?

This means that the mortgage payoff balance is higher than the fair market value of your property. This situation is on the other end of the spectrum. In North America, out of all the properties with mortgages, 22.5 percent of the properties are in negative equity positions. And this percentage continues to increase due to the large volume of properties flooding the market. As more properties are added to the market on a monthly basis, in part due to foreclosures, the law of supply and demand will dictate the market value of the properties.

This would be the worst situation for a homeowner. However, there is hope! Depending on how flexible the bank collections agent is, or how desperate the bank is to remove your property from the NPA[3] list, there is a strategy that you could use to get out of this situation with little damage to your credit record and maybe even with a few dollars in your pocket. In fact, the very purpose of this book is to show you how it could be done. I will go into further detail in Chapters 5 and 6.

Again, this 22.5 percent is the national average and depending in which state your property is located, the percentage may be higher or

---

[3] Non-preforming asset

lower. In addition, as more and more foreclosed properties flood the market, I anticipate the percentage of properties with negative equity will increase even more. As more foreclosed properties flood the market, the price of real estate will continue to drop. Unfortunately, there appears to be no end in sight for this phenomenon.

Rules of the game

Substantial progress in any field of endeavor is impossible in the absence of the working knowledge of the basic rules of the game. In real estate, there are two basic rules and as you begin to analyze the information and consider your options, you must learn the working basics.

Before you start to consider your options and the strategy that you will use to approach your current financial situation, it is important to point out the first rule in real estate: **Everything is negotiable** and I mean *everything*. When you start to consider your options, you must have this rule at the forefront of any idea that comes to mind. Do not limit the possibilities by what you would consider possible or impossible. I will say it again, everything is negotiable. Some things to consider include, but are not limited to, price reduction, interest rate reduction and a portion of the mortgage balance being forgiven.

In order for me to illustrate the second rule in real estate, play along with me and follow my instructions. Perhaps you may consider it childish; nevertheless, please humor me. I am trying to prove a point and once you learn it, it will serve you well in your future negotiations with your lending institution.

Take the book along with you so that you can follow the instructions that I will be giving you. Before you read any further, find yourself a large mirror, either in a bedroom or bathroom and stand in front of the mirror. Now that you are standing in front of the mirror, stand on your right leg. Now with your right hand touch your left ear, now count to three and at the count of three yell 'yahoo' at the top of your lungs. Stay there, do not go anywhere, and look at the reflection of the image in the mirror and ask yourself. Why did I do that? What on earth prompted me to do something so silly?

The answer is … **because I asked you to do it**, and this is the point that I wanted to make. No one in his or her right mind will do something so silly, but you just did, and you looked somewhat silly doing it. Why did you do it? Because I asked. You will be surprised by what people will do for you, if you just ask. This is rule number two and this rule does not only apply to real estate; you can use it in every aspect of your life: "**Never be afraid to ask for what you want.**"

One final point before we start to consider your options. Whenever an idea comes to mind, or when you ask something from someone, you must ask yourself the following three questions:

- What would be the best thing that could happen? If they comply with your request, that would be the best thing that could happen.

- What would be the worst thing that could happen? If they decline your request, that would be the worst thing that could happen. That only brings you to where you are now and that is not *that* bad. You are still in the same place had you not made the request or asked the question.

- What would be the most likely thing that could happen? The most likely thing that could happen may be that you end up somewhere between a flat-out rejection and the complete acceptance of your request. In reality, any movement in the direction of your request is a gain for you. Anything the other party is willing to give you, would be more than what you had before you asked the question.

Consider the most likely result to your request and if that is acceptable to you, then you are able to proceed with confidence, free from fear or worry. Because now your intellectual understanding tells you that the worst thing that could happen will most likely not happen and you will be moving in the right direction, the direction of your goal, whatever the request may be.

Make a list of what you know

Before you even consider making an appointment with the bank's lending officer, you must make a physical checklist of all the facts that you have gathered up until now and collect the supporting documents that go along with it. I strongly suggest that you create a file folder with the checklist and supporting documents and bring them along with you when you go to speak with the lending officer.

This is a list of items that you should have in your file folder:

From the legal advisor:

- Your rights and obligations under the law

- Where you are in the foreclosure process

- How much time you have remaining to sell your house or to work out an alternate arrangement with your lending officer.

From the lending institution:

- The exact payoff amount that you owe the bank, including late fees, legal fees, prepayment penalties and any other fees that may apply.

From the real estate broker:

- A real estate market evaluation of the fair market value of your property

- How much you can sell your house for and how long it will take to sell

- Determine which of the three situations you are in based on the market evaluation (for example: upside down, breaking even or ahead).

From your income and expense sheet:

- Total income and household expenses

- List of creditors and minimum monthly payments

Now that we have all this information in an organized format, we are going to think of different ways you can approach your particular situation and create different strategies to present to your lending officer when you go out to meet them.

I have no way of knowing what your financial picture is like, but in the next chapters I will give you a few different strategies that you can modify to suit your particular financial situation.

Problem Solving Strategies

I would like to teach you a technique that I learned when I was in school on how to solve any problem that comes your way.

Step number one:

- Take a blank sheet of paper, lined is best, and at the top of the sheet write the heading "GIVEN." Under the word given, write all the facts that you have gathered up to this point.

- Next, you will have the heading "REQUIRED." Before you start to think of strategies to solve your problem, you need to have a goal. You need to know your preferred outcome. What is it that you require? What do you want? I can't stress this point enough; you need to know what you want as an outcome before you start to think of possible solutions. How can you find a solution to your problem if you don't know what you want?

- Lastly you will have the heading "SOLUTION." Here you will develop your ideas and strategies to solve your problem.

Someone once said that "an identified problem is half solved" and I agree with that statement. If you have followed my instructions, you are halfway there. By now you have all the facts in front of you, you have gathered the information, you have identified any additional information that you will require and have determined what you want the outcome to be. Now all you need to do is to find the solution.

> *"If you can tell me what you want,*
> *I can show you how to get it"*
> **—Bob Proctor**

In my personal experience, the biggest challenge that you will encounter is to find out what it is that you really want. Once you identify what it is that you really want, the solution to your situation will almost solve itself.

This concept has a biblical foundation. In chapter ten in the book of Mark, there is the story of a blind man named Bartimaeus. Mark 10:47 states, *"And when he heard that it was Jesus the Nazarene, he began to cry out and say, Jesus, Son of David, have mercy on me!"* In this verse, Bartimaeus is asking for mercy. The word mercy is too broad; it could mean different things to different people depending on their need. The Lord Jesus had to refocus Bartimaeus and asked him a question; tell me in a single sentence what type of mercy do you want me to have on you?

Mark 10:51 goes on to say, *"And Jesus answered him and said, what do you want Me to do for you? And the blind man said to Him, Rabboni, that I may receive my sight."* Once Bartimaeus was able to describe in a single sentence what he wanted, the Lord Jesus responded to his request.

Mark 10:52 continues, *"And Jesus said to him, Go; your faith has healed you. And immediately he received his sight and followed Him on the road."*

What do you really want as the solution to your problem? You must have a clear picture in your mind as to what you want. You should be able to tell your lending officer **in a single sentence** what you want. Failing to come up with a single statement describing what it is that you want will hinder you from moving forward. Learn from the story of Bartimaeus; he was clear about what he wanted and he got exactly what he asked for.

In your particular case, it may be that you want more than one thing. List them all, fill out those columns I mentioned above. Make a full list of things and once you identify them all, prioritize them. Give the most pressing item the highest ranking and then work your way down the list. You will be happily surprised as to what the outcome of this simple exercise can do for you.

Once you have identified what it is that you want, get to work. You have all the information you need, and you have identified the additional information you require to solve your problem.

Chapter 5
Results of the Financial Analysis

AFTER GOING THROUGH the exercise of analyzing your financial situation and identifying the main cause of your problem, you should have a clear picture of where you are financially and what you should do to correct the problem. How did you fare?

As mentioned previously, you can find yourself in one of three possible situations. You could be *ahead, breaking even* or *underwater*. Let's take a look at each one of these possible conditions to determine what defense strategy will work best for you.

What could you do if you are ahead?

Since you have done your homework and have gathered all your personal financial information along with the information related to your property, you should have been able to easily verify that your mortgage balance is less than the fair market value of your property. As mentioned in the previous chapter, this is the best situation that you can find yourself in.

In addition, since you analyzed your personal financial information by creating an income and expense sheet, you will have been able to determine the reason for your inability to make your mortgage payments.

Whatever the reason, you have fallen behind on your mortgage payments and since it is impossible for me to know your specific financial situation or the reason why you have fallen behind on your payments, I am simply going to assume that there is a good reason for it. Perhaps you have lost your job, or fallen ill, or a close family member has become sick, and you needed to care for that person.

Regardless of the reason, the fact remains the same, you have fallen behind on your mortgage payments and the bank is threatening to foreclose on your property, and if you do not take action, you are in danger of losing your home.

If you do not take action quickly, on top of your regular mortgage payment, the bank will add all the fees that they can think of, and since there is equity in your property, the lending officer may be less willing to help you or forgive the additional charges. You will soon find out that the banks late fees and legal fees add up very quickly. If you do not take some form of quick action, the fees will eat away a large portion of the equity in your house and it will cost you even more money to settle your account later.

What options are available to you and what strategies should you use in this particular case? Again, since it is impossible for me to know your particular situation, you need to figure this out for yourself and determine what strategy will work best in your case, based on what you really want.

If you have lost the ability to generate income due to illness or a layoff, you need to consider your situation. If it is a short-term problem, you may be able to handle it quickly and easily by soliciting help from family and friends. If it is a long-term problem, you may have to take a different approach. This is a very important consideration that you need to take into account and it must be looked at with a clear and sober mind. As an example, let's suppose that you have been laid off from your job. You may think that this is a short-term problem and perhaps it is. You may be saying, "When I get a job, everything will be ok." When are you going to get a job? What are you doing to get a new job? Is the company that laid you off going to hire you back? What are the prospects for new employment? These are serious questions that you must ask yourself. Make a plan and prepare yourself for the worst-case scenario.

At the moment you may consider your situation a short-term problem, however, if there are no new prospects for employment opportunities, nine months down the road you will discover that it was not a short-term problem at all. Because you believed your situation was a short-term problem, you may be so deep in the hole that it would be impossible for you to get out. You must consider this matter of a short-term or long-term problem under the proper light so that you can identify the problem early on and take proper action.

If you do not have any friends or family that can help you financially, the next best option will be to talk to the bank's lending officer and explain your situation. Ask them if they would be willing to put the missed payments at the back end of the mortgage. What this means is that they will add the missed payments to the principle amount of the loan. Eventually you will have to pay for the missed mortgage payments, but that will not happen until the end of the mortgage term.

In addition, it will cost you more in interest because now you are paying interest on the additional amount that was added to the back of the mortgage. The advantage of this strategy is that you no longer have to worry about coming up with the funds to cover the late payments, not to mention that you just saved your house from going into foreclosure.

Another short-term option is to talk to the bank's lending officer and arrange a late mortgage repayment plan. This plan can be spread out over a number of months and as long as you honor your repayment agreement there will be no further action taken against you.

Another possibility is to contact a different lending institution and try to obtain alternate financing, either by refinancing your house or by obtaining a line of credit that will cover the late payments and give you enough liquidity to live on until your financial situation improves.

This last strategy will work in both short and long-term situations. Put your house on the market. I know that you do not want to hear this, but it is an option that is available to you. You know how much your house is worth; you know how much you can sell it for, and how long it will take to sell. If you want to sell it quickly, you may consider lowering the price by a few thousand dollars to encourage a quick sale.

Since you completed your homework in the previous chapter, you have a very good idea of how much cash you will put in your pocket once the house is sold. At this point, you may be asking yourself, what is the benefit in doing that? I can list *at least* three good reasons:

- You will walk away with cash in your pocket, and if you are facing financial challenges, the cash will help you settle down until things turn around in your favor.

- You will have saved your house from going into foreclosure, eliminated the risk of losing everything including the equity in your house, and most likely have avoided losing your life savings as well.

- You will have saved your credit record, and this is one of the most important reasons why you should consider this option. It is more difficult to repair your credit after a foreclosure than after declaring bankruptcy. Your house is your most precious material possession and if you walk away from it, you will have no problem walking away from any lesser loan obligations in the future. The bank will refuse to take that risk with you again if you allow your house to be foreclosed on.

I know that selling your home is not the most appealing solution, due to your emotional attachment to your property. However, if you do not take some action, the bank will take away your home, sell it for you, and give you nothing in return. At the very least, with this option, you are walking away with cash in your pocket. The decision to sell gives you some control of the situation. You are the one making the decision to sell your home, not the bank. Do not allow the bank to make that decision for you.

If you, in fact, choose to sell your home, the first thing that you must do is emotionally detach yourself from your property. Failing to remove yourself emotionally from your property will cloud your judgment and it will hinder you from making a logical decision. In your eyes, your property is your home, the place where you feel safe and secure, and/or the place where you may have raised your children. It has sentimental value and there are strong emotions attached to your property for many possible reasons. However, to the bank, your home is only a house, a physical structure. If you are going to be successful in detaching yourself emotionally from your property, I strongly suggest that you start to see your home as a physical structure where you live.

Unless you are able to come up with a better solution, I encourage you to just let it go and put the property on the market. Afterwards, once you are back on your feet financially, and if the property still means that much to you, you can always go back and try to buy your old home.

I remember when we were going through our own foreclosure nightmare. I had to tell my family that we had lost the house and that we had to move out; my second daughter was only nine years old at the time. She came to me in tears, telling me that she loved our house and that she did not want to move out. She told me, "I love this house, this is my home, and I don't want to move." It broke my heart to pieces, but by that time a court order had already been issued and we only had a few days to gather all of our belongings and move or we would be forcibly removed.

As tears ran down her cheeks, I made her a promise. I told her that one day we would have a much better house and that, if she wanted, we could come back and buy this house back. She responded by telling me that she did not want a better house, she loved *that* house. Unfortunately, staying in that house was not an option at the time. Seven years later, I kept that promise. We bought a much better house and thankfully, she did not insist on buying the old house back. Did we love that house? Yes, at the time we did. We still have many fond memories of that house and of the time we spent living there but we have carried on with our lives.

I am sharing this painful experience with you to encourage and show you that even if you end up losing your home, it is not the end of the world. You will survive and life will go on. By reading this book, my hope is that you will successfully be able to defend your home and will not go through the same experience my family and I went through many years ago.

An important thing to note is that in most states there is a 'foreclosure redemption' law. It states, "A person that has lost a property to a foreclosure has the right to buy the property back from the current owner." Some states give you one to five years, while other states give you an unlimited amount of time to redeem your property. Your legal adviser should be able to give you more information as to the statutes of the law in your particular state of residence.

What could you do if you are breaking even?

If this is your situation, you are like the proverbial saying, stuck between a rock and a hard place. Based on the information that you gathered, you have determined that the fair market value of your house is about the same as your mortgage balance. Your situation is not unique; in fact, 29 percent of fellow homeowners are in the same predicament.

Before we go into developing a strategy for this situation, have you considered the possibility of cutting down on some of your expenses to help free up some funds to make up your monthly income deficit? Double-check your income and expense sheet, and identify monthly expenses that could be cut down or reduced without causing you too much hardship. However, if you are already on a tight budget, we will need to consider different strategies.

What strategy could you use in this situation? Again, you must determine if your financial situation is a short-term problem or a long-term problem. If it is a short-term problem as mentioned previously, you can ask family and/or friends for financial assistance and, as a last resort, you can approach the bank's lending officer and arrange a repayment plan for your late payments, fees, and additional interest charges.

If it is a long-term problem, based on the information you have gathered, you know how much you can sell your house for and how long it will take to sell it. If you are seeking a quick sale, you will need to lower the price. However, if you lower the price of your home, and since there is no equity in your house, after the sale you will end up with a mortgage deficit that you will need to repay the bank.

Now this may be an option worth considering. If the deficit amount is something that you can live with, maybe you should consider selling your house, and after the house is sold you can make a payment arrangement plan with the bank.

In your case, the lending officer will be less willing to add the late payments to the back end of the mortgage. However, you can always ask. Remember rule number two: *You will be surprised as to what people will do for you if you simply ask.*

What if you were to ask the bank collection agent to lower the interest rate on your mortgage so that you are better able to manage your payments?

What if you ask the bank collection agent for a longer amortization period to lower your monthly payments? Remember that the bank does not want to take away your home. All they want is for you to keep making the regular monthly payments so that they will have consistent revenue from your property. You really need to create a list of 'what if' scenarios to come up with a good solution to your problem.

What if you calculated that the mortgage deficit is too high for you to consider selling your house? Since many people are losing their homes and are being evicted from their properties, these people need to live somewhere. Some can move in with relatives, but the great majority, especially families with children, will need to get their own rental place. Therefore, there is a very good chance that you will be able to rent or lease your property much quicker than if you put your property on the market. You can rent a portion of your property like a basement suite or rent out the entire house. The only requirement on your part will be to make sure that the rent amount you collect is more than your mortgage payment.

What would be the benefit of using this option? Firstly, someone else will be making your mortgage payments. Secondly, you could move in with a friend of family member until you get back on your feet again, or you can go out and rent a smaller place.

I am throwing out all of these ideas so that you can see that there are many different options for you to consider. Also, keep in mind the first rule in real estate—*everything is negotiable*. If you manage to negotiate a payment reduction plan with your bank's lending officer, and you decide to rent a portion of your house or rent the entire place, you may end up with a couple hundred dollars in your pocket at the end of every month from the rent you are collecting. This money you are collecting from your tenants serves as an additional source of income. This will come in handy if you are on a tight budget.

You could also create a lease-to-own agreement on your property. By asking the tenant for a deposit, and giving them an option to purchase your property from you at a later date, you will end up with cash in your *back pocket*. In the next chapter, I will go into more detail about the structure of a lease-to-own agreement.

What could you do if you are underwater?

From your fact-finding mission you discovered that your property is underwater, and as mentioned earlier, this is the worst situation that you can find yourself in. Although only 22.5 percent of properties with mortgages in North America are being affected, the numbers are unprecedented and causing many banks substantial losses.

What this means in real numbers, on a national level, is that for every 100 properties with mortgages there are 22.5 properties underwater. This does not mean that 22.5 percent of the properties are in foreclosure. It simply means that the value of the property is lower than the homeowners current mortgage balance. It means that if all the people that are underwater stop making payments on their properties, many more banks will go under and there is no way for the banks to save themselves from such losses.

However, at a local level in some areas of the country the numbers are much higher. The state of Nevada is one example. Out of all the properties with mortgages in Nevada, 50 percent are underwater meaning they have a negative equity in their property. That means one out of every two properties is suffering the effect of this phenomenon. The numbers are mind boggling, and with such numbers, it is no surprise that banks are failing.

There are two types of homeowners, the first type of homeowner does not have a job, and they are facing tremendous financial challenges and emotional distress. If you fall into this category of homeowner, and do not have an income, it is very difficult to meet your basic needs. Every day becomes a challenge and struggle to feed your family and the last thing on your mind is to give the last few dollars in your pocket to the bank. You are in survival mode, and every day you must choose between feeding your family and making the mortgage payment.

The second type of homeowners are the ones who do have a regular job or a steady stream of income, but their homes have dropped in value so much so that they have simply stopped making their regular mortgage payments. They have decided that it is not worth paying for something that is overpriced. Instead of taking the time to talk to their lending officer and negotiate a mortgage balance reduction or any other type of solution, they abandon their property.

Let us consider the second type of homeowner in more detail. These homeowners are facing a huge dilemma in regards to their property. Should they keep making the mortgage payments although they are fully aware that their house is worth less than the fair market value, or should they walk away from their financial obligation with the bank? Unfortunately, many homeowners have chosen to walk away from their obligations, allowing the bank to take away their home. Their thoughts are governed by the current reality of the real estate market. However, if their thoughts are governed by principle, they would realize that at some point in time, the real estate market will turn around. In fact, in some places in the USA and Canada, the real estate market has already begun to do so. Therefore, instead of walking away, they should talk to the bank and negotiate a mortgage balance reduction, interest rate reduction or something that it is fair and acceptable to all parties involved.

These homeowners have made an unwise choice; they have made a poor decision, and it will affect their lives for many years to come. If you find yourself in this situation, first, seek professional, legal advice. At the very least find out what the consequences will be to your credit record and find out if that is your only choice. Get informed first, and then decide what the best course of action is for your personal situation. Please do not make a rushed decision, and do not walk away from your obligations without weighing all of your options or without considering the consequences first.

The homeowners that are underwater have fallen into a trap, and there is no easy way out. They can't sell their home at a discounted price because there is no equity and they can't give it away because no one will want to buy something for more than the fair market value. Even if they find someone willing to buy the house at an inflated price, the bank will not approve a new mortgage for the potential buyer because the property is worth less than the new loan amount.

Before we go any further, let me remind you of the importance of a good credit rating in the North American society. You can't even rent a carpet cleaning machine without a credit card. Walking away from your mortgage obligation will give your credit record such a black stain that it will take many years to amend. I urge you to seek professional advice before making any decision. Whatever decision you make will affect your financial future in more than one way for a very long time. Additionally, if you maintain a decent credit score, when the economy turns around it will be much easier for you to get back on your feet. Instead of being entangled in cleaning up your credit mess, you will be able to take advantage of financial opportunities that will arise.

What can you do? Should you continue making your mortgage payments or abandon the property? Is there a way out of this situation, where both the homeowner and the bank come out ahead without going into foreclosure or at the very least minimize your losses? Can you turn this into a win-win situation?

The answer is yes, there is always something that can be done in this case. However, it will require much preparation on your part, great negotiation skills, and a very motivated mortgage collection agent. In the current market situation, there are many motivated mortgage collection agents out there who are willing to bend over backwards in order for you to uphold your mortgage obligation. They do not want you to walk away from your mortgage obligation, especially when the mortgage is upside down.

How do we approach this particular situation? Earlier in the book I mentioned the importance of gathering information, and I will stress it again. Before you can even think about strategies that will help you solve the problem, you **MUST** have accurate and well documented information regarding your particular case. You will require all of this information to be able to present it as evidence when you go to speak to your mortgage collection agent. The entire next chapter is dedicated to ideas and strategies homeowners can use to find a plausible solution for the *upside down* (or underwater) mortgage situation.

Chapter 6
Underwater Strategies

WHAT CAN YOU do if you are underwater? I guess it will all depend on how deep underwater you find yourself in. As mentioned before, this is the worst financial situation that you can find yourself in.

How bad is it? Let's consider the worst possible situation as an example. Let's say that you are two months late on your mortgage payment because you lost your job, the unemployment insurance check does not cover all of your expenses, and your savings account is completely empty. You have maxed-out all of your credit cards and you can no longer make the minimum monthly credit card payments. Furthermore, your house has lost 50 percent in value and you are locked in at a 5.5 percent interest mortgage rate, and to make the situation even worse, your car just broke down! I am not sure that it could get *any* worse than this.

This example may sound like a joke, but this is the reality that many families are experiencing as we speak. I really hope this is not your case. However, if this is your case or a variation of something similar, you may be asking yourself: Is there anything that can be done? The answer is **yes**, there is something that can be done. The first thing that you need to do is to sit down and analyze the information that you have gathered in order to bring clarity to your specific situation.

Personal finances

Before you go any further, you must consider the matter of your personal financial picture. The first step that you need to take is to go over your income and household expenses. Try to identify unnecessary expenses that you can eliminate or drastically reduce. We all have those little expenses that we never consider as expenses, but at the end of the month, they all add up. Let's take a cup of coffee as an example. If you have a cup of Starbucks coffee every day, and I am talking coffee, not the more expensive lattes, you are spending over $50.00 a month on coffee alone. That represents $600.00 per year. Could you use an additional $600.00 a year? That is for a single cup of coffee a day. There are people that have two or three cups of Starbucks coffee a day. The real question becomes: Are you willing to sacrifice a cup of Starbucks coffee a day to save the roof over your head? I hope the answer is YES!

Go over every item on the income and expense sheet and try to find a way to cut down your expenses.

Another area that you should look at includes household items purchased on credit from a department store. As you well know, all department stores charge the borderline usury rate of 29.9 percent. If you have purchased something from a department store on credit, and this item is something that you do not use, (like a treadmill machine) find out if you can return it to get a refund. If the return period has expired, see if you can sell it on e-bay or Craigslist and use that money to pay off the credit card that is eating away at your money. Believe me, at 29.9 percent interest, you will never finish paying off that credit card.

As for your house, what can you do to improve the situation? You are in a very difficult situation because you can't give your house away. No one in their right mind will want to buy something for more than what it is worth, and as the saying goes, *"it is not a bargain at any price."* In fact it is such a rotten deal that not even the bank wants it back!

What can you do in such a grim situation? In this type of circumstance, there is no *single* strategy that you can use. However, a *combination* of strategies can be employed to improve the situation and may be even improve the circumstances to such an extent that you may come up ahead.

In this example what is the problem? The problem is that you do not have a job, your unemployment income is barely enough to cover your basic living expenses and you are not at all excited about paying for a house that is worth less than the mortgage balance. Remember the purpose of this book is to help you defend your house from a foreclosure procedure and at the same time to preserve your good credit standing. If your house has dropped 50 percent in value and your interest rate is locked in at 5.5 percent, the situation may seem hopeless and you may feel that it is too much of a burden to bear. It does not make any sense from a financial standpoint to continue making payments on something that it is not worth the price. Nevertheless, the last thing that you want to consider doing is to walk away from your debt obligations. You are better than that.

Worst-case scenario

Before we get into the details of how to generate strategies for this particular situation, let's take one step back and consider the seriousness of your financial situation. You know that you are in deep financial trouble. Now, I am going to ask you to close your eyes and consider what would be the very worst thing that could happen to you. For the sake of illustration, let's suppose that the worst thing that could happen to you is that the bailiff comes to your house and forcefully removes you from your property and throws all of your belongings on the side of the road. In my mind that would be the worst thing that could happen to anyone.

Now consider, on a scale of one to ten, what are the real chances of that event taking place? Now, keep this in mind as you begin to think of strategies to defend your home—*any improvement that you can make on the worst-case scenario while negotiating with the bank is a gain for you.*

Mortgage interest and balance reduction

Let's consider some ideas that you could employ. What if you ask your bank collection agent to renegotiate a lower interest rate on the balance of your mortgage? Would that help you avoid foreclosure? Remember that in real estate, **everything is negotiable** and since you have done your due diligence in gathering all of your personal finances and gathered information on the current market value of your property, you can show the collection agent hard evidence of what you are referring to. If they are willing to lower the interest rate on the balance of the mortgage, you can continue to make the mortgage payments.

What other concessions could you ask the bank to make? What about a 50 percent reduction in the balance of the mortgage? You have the evidence that the property has lost 50 percent of its value. What if you ask your bank collection agent to forgive 50 percent of the loan, or any portion of the loan? This would be a huge step forward, it is impossible for them to argue against the facts and you have all the evidence to prove it. Furthermore, you had nothing to do with your property's dramatic drop in value. It is a reality of the current real estate market, and you are a victim, as well as the bank, of the foreclosure phenomenon.

Why would the bank even contemplate such a ridiculous offer? If the lending officer stops to consider your offer, they will determine, based on the information that you have provided them, and based on their own research, that your offer is the best offer that they will receive.

Consider the banks options for a moment. What are their options? In reality, they only have two options. Option one is to scare you into making up the late payments and then frighten you into consistently making your mortgage payments until the full mortgage amount is paid in full. However, both you and the bank know that the first option is no longer an option. Their second best option is to continue the foreclosure process and, as mentioned earlier, that is the last thing the bank wants to do. Both are very powerful reasons and it is not in the bank's best interest to continue with the foreclosure process.

If the bank chooses to continue with the foreclosure process, it will take six to eight months for the bank to obtain a court order to take back possession of your house. That means that they will not receive a single mortgage payment during that time. That reason alone represents a few thousand dollars in lost revenue for the bank, but it is not the most compelling reason for them to agree to drop the loan amount by 50 percent. During the foreclosure process there will be additional expenses such as court filing fees, lawyer fees, etc. As you know, lawyers are not cheap and they have a tendency to charge astronomical fees, which the bank will have to pay. This will represent additional losses totaling a few more thousand dollars.

The bank will threaten to sue you in order to recover the court filing and lawyer fees. However, if the bank sues you for the deficiency on your loan, you can declare bankruptcy. In such a case the bank will have to absorb the losses and they will not be able to recover any money from you at that point. This has been a very hard lesson the banks have learned over the last few years. They have forced people out of their homes and then tried to sue them for the mortgage deficiency and fees with the belief that they could recover all of their losses. Due to their hard-nosed attitude towards the homeowner, when the homeowner is sued for thousands of dollars in a mortgage deficiency lawsuit, the homeowner has no other choice but to declare bankruptcy and the bank has ended up with nothing more than a tax write-off. This has now become something the banks want to avoid.

Once the bank takes possession of the property and you are out of the house, the bank still needs to spend more money to hire a managing company to take care of the property, continue to pay for all of the utilities, pay property insurance, and hire a realtor to sell the property. These are significant expenses, with the realtor fees alone being a few thousand dollars. Not to mention that the property can and most likely will sit on the market for months due to the huge number of properties for sale. The bank will not receive any revenue related to that property during this time, which increases their financial losses by a few more thousand dollars. Are you beginning to see the pattern here? Do you have a better understanding of why the bank would not want to do this?

The most compelling reason why a bank may be willing to forgive 50 percent of your loan amount is the current market value of the property. When the bank lists the property, what do you think the listing price will be? The listing price will have to be the fair market value of the property. If they choose to ask for more than the property is worth, no one will want to purchase the property. If they want a quick sale, they may have to lower the listing price further below the market value. This is their reality and a compelling reason to consider your offer. Again, they will threaten you with a deficiency judgment, and they know better. If you are forced to go bankrupt, the bank will be unable to recover any of their losses.

Now that I have listed all the expenses that the bank will have to incur, it may be clear to you that the offer you presented to the bank is a reasonable offer. You are offering them 50 cents on the dollar, where if they were to reject your offer and continue with the foreclosure process, they may count themselves lucky to get 35 cents on the dollar for your property.

Sometimes the bank-lending officer is a young, eager new college graduate and may not know all of the consequences in rejecting your offer. It then becomes your responsibility to educate him using the well documented evidence that you have gathered. Once he becomes fully aware of the consequences, he may be more willing to consider your offer. Make the situation clear to the bank that it is in the bank's best interest to work out a solution with you, rather than to continue with the foreclosure process.

I hope that by now you are getting excited about the information that I have shared with you. The great majority of homeowners do not know this and they end up losing their home and damaging their credit for many years. Remember, when it comes to real estate, *everything is negotiable.* You must ask for what you want and you will be surprised to see what people will do for you, just because you asked.

By negotiating a new mortgage agreement with your bank, you have lowered your debt, lowered the interest rate on your mortgage, and lowered your monthly mortgage payments. If the new mortgage payment is something that you can live with, then your problem is solved. Furthermore, you have saved further deterioration towards your credit record.

Creating new income

If the bank agrees to forgive a portion of your mortgage balance to bring it to par with the current market value of the property, your situation has improved, and you have moved up a notch. Now you are in a break-even position and you can use the same strategies listed under that heading in the previous chapter.

What about your income? Let's suppose that you have lost your job and there are no signs of a new job prospect. How are you going to keep your new mortgage agreement with the bank if you have no income? They bent backwards to accommodate your needs, and now you must honor that agreement. You will be hard pressed to keep your agreement with the bank and no matter how much you want to make good on your promise, you will not be able to do it. In fact, the collection agent will be reluctant to agree to any balance reduction or interest rate reduction if you are not able to prove to them that you will be able to manage the new mortgage payments. This matter is something that you need to have an answer for when you go to see the bank collection agent. How are you going to make the mortgage payments? You need to show the bank concrete evidence that you will be able to honor the agreement.

A simple solution is to rent out a room or a basement suite in your house to generate additional income to help cover some expenses. Remember, many homeowners are losing their homes, and that has created a huge demand for rental units. The rental market is booming just about anywhere you are in the country.

Another suggestion is to rent or lease out your entire property while you move in with a family member or a friend. Another possibility is to rent a smaller place, just until you are able to secure a stable source of income. Because your house is bigger than an apartment unit, the rent amount that you will collect from your house will be higher than the rent you will pay for an apartment, thus creating positive cash flow every month. This money can be used to supplement your income.

Lease-to-own for profit

At the beginning of this book, I mentioned that I was going to show you a strategy that could help you get out from under an upside down situation and even put some money in your pocket. I also mentioned that there was no *single* strategy that would work for this situation, but a *combination* of strategies could be used. Here it comes.

Assuming that you were successful in negotiating a lower interest rate with the bank, and reduced the total loan amount on your mortgage, both simple strategies combined have reduced your monthly mortgage payments significantly. Furthermore, you were also successful in defending your home and you prevented the foreclosure procedure to continue, which would have brought financial ruin to you and your family.

Now we must further consider the matter of your income. If your cash inflow has not improved and your cash reserve has been depleted, you will have the same problem in the very near future. If you do not find a new source of income soon or a way to supplement your income, in a few short months you will be in the same predicament.

Below is an option worth considering and as mentioned earlier, the rental market is booming with people who have lost their properties and are now out looking for a place to live or a way to acquire a new home. However, the damage caused to their credit record by the foreclosure process will hinder them from getting a new mortgage. The bank has lost tens of thousands of dollars foreclosing on their property and they will not be willing to forgive that offense easily.

These former homeowners are finding out the hard way the consequences of walking away from their obligation with the bank. Many of these former homeowners have found new employment, many of them have good incomes, but they are trying very hard to re-establish their credit record, but no lending institution will grant them credit for at least several years. This is an unwritten code of honor among these lending institutions.

The majority of people, who have lost their properties, are not all bad people. They were responsible law abiding citizens, paying all of their bills on time when they were caught in the financial crises. They lost their only source of income, they panicked, they failed to get the information that you now possess and consequently they lost their property and their good credit standing. For example, I know an oil company executive that was caught right in the middle of the financial crises. The company he was employed with slowed down to such an extent that they had to lay him off and he could not find another job. About nine months later, the company that he was working for rehired him, but by this time the damage to his credit had already been done. He had lost his house and his credit along with it. He is a good person, and since then he has regained employment and has been working diligently to pay back all his creditors. When I met him he had been working at it for two years. After I spoke with a mortgage broker about his situation, the mortgage broker told me that even though the gentleman in question had been working diligently to re-establish his credit, there would be at least another two years before any bank would even offer him a second chance. Additionally, once the bank decides to give this former homeowner a second chance, he will need to come up with a higher down payment and the interest rate the bank will charge him will be much higher than the going rate.

I can't stress enough the importance of defending your property from going into foreclosure. It will cost you greatly for a very long time if you allow this to occur.

Since there is an abundance of people in these types of situations, why couldn't you create a way to help each other out?

There is a strategy that will work brilliantly in this situation. On the one hand, you may or may not have a job or a source of income. Although you were successful in negotiating a lower interest rate and reduction in your mortgage balance, your income may not be sufficient to cover all of your expenses.

Please give this idea some thought. Would you consider moving your family in with a friend or a family member for one or two years? Or would you consider moving into an apartment for one or two years? In addition, rent out your house for the same length of time. Is this idea something that you will even consider? I am fully aware of the different lifestyle you must endure in a rental unit, but due to the reality of your financial situation will this be a sacrifice you are willing to make?

Somewhere there is a person that is seeking a second chance at homeownership—someone that has a good income, with a steady job, but with a poor credit record due to a previous foreclosure. Why couldn't you create a lease-to-own agreement with this person seeking a second chance? They will be helping you make your mortgage payments and at the same time, it will create a positive cash flow for you to make-up your income deficit.

Why would this 'second chance homeowner' even consider such an option? In reality, he doesn't have another option. His next best option is to keep renting until the bank decides that he deserves another chance, which could be several years in the future. If you have ever lived in an apartment complex unit, you will agree that it is not the best place to raise a family.

First, you must understand what a lease-to-own agreement is. A lease-to-own agreement means that your tenant has the option to purchase your property at any time on or before the expiration date of the lease agreement term. In the lease-to-own option, you and the tenant agree on the length of the term and the price of the property. The agreed upon price does not have to be the current market price of the property, you must agree on the future purchase price of the property and that will be determined by the length of the term. If you agree on a one year term, then the price will be closer to the current market value of the property. However, if the length of the term is three or even four years, the future price of the property will most likely increase. No one knows with exact certainty where the property price will be in three or four years down the road, but if you take the country's current rate of inflation as a guide, it will tell you that the property should increase in value to keep pace with the current rate of inflation.

How does this work? As an example, let's say that the current price of your property is $150,000.00. Regardless of your current house value, the principle is the same whether the price of the property is lower or higher, and I am fully aware that in some cities you can't even buy a single car garage for that price. Using the $150,000.00 current value of the property, you agree on a 3-year lease-to-own term with a 3% per year rate of inflation, you should be asking for at least $163,900.00 as the future purchase price.

In this example it may seem as though you are taking advantage of the credit challenged future homeowner, but you are not, because the price is well in the future—$163,900.00 is a reasonable purchase price. You may be thinking, what if home prices drop further down? How much further down can they go? What if the price goes up to $200,000.00, would you feel the same way then?

Remember that nothing in this world travels in a straight line, nothings goes straight up or straight down forever. The real estate market at some point in time will turn around. Those are life cycles and real estate prices are not immune to them. The laws of the universe are governed by these laws. Just as the tides in the ocean go up, they must go down; this is how the universe operates. If you apply this principle to the current real estate market, you know that at some point in time, the market will turn around. We don't know when that will take place, but we know that it will do so.

What would be the benefit to you in creating a lease-to-own agreement? The first and most important benefit is that you do not have to come up with your mortgage payments every month. This fact alone will save you a great deal of stress and alleviate a large amount of your financial pressure. It will help save your credit record from any further damage. It will create a much needed positive cash flow condition and it will put some cash in your pocket.

Cash in your pocket? I know I have not talked about this in great detail yet. You will find a few guidelines in Appendix D on how to structure a lease-to-own agreement.

I will briefly explain how you will be able to put cash in your pocket. When you arrange a lease-to-own agreement, there will be two aspects to the agreement. One is the rental aspect of the property; the other is the actual lease-to-own section. These are two separate agreements. The first agreement covers the standard rental agreement, the rental amount, security deposit, and rights and responsibilities of both the tenant and the property owner.

The second agreement is a separate agreement where the details of the lease-to-own particulars are specified. Here you will stipulate the length of the term, what will constitute a breach in the contract, the consequences of breaching the contract and the down payment on the property.

You will find details on how to structure a lease-to-own agreement in Appendix D. One item that I would like to point out and make very clear to you is the matter of the down payment. The down payment on the house is not, I repeat, **is not** the security deposit. The security deposit is the money that you receive for the rental part of the agreement. The down payment is the money that you will receive as a down payment for your property, and this money must be paid up front.

You must insist on getting at least a five percent deposit for the down payment on the agreed future purchase price of your property. You do not know the potential homebuyer of your property and under what conditions they lost their home. For all you know they might have just walked away from their obligation with the bank. Please, always keep in mind that if the bank is not willing to take a chance on them, you should also proceed cautiously. You must protect your interest at all times and the best way for you to do this is by insisting on *at least* a five percent down payment up front. As mentioned earlier, once the bank decides to give them a second chance, they will have to come up with a higher down payment. Also, the interest rate that the bank will charge them on the new mortgage will be much higher than the going rate. Why would this second chance homeowner be willing to accept such abuse from the bank? If they want to own a home again, they have no other choice.

Now you are giving them a second chance to become a homeowner again. If they refuse to give you something as a deposit for the down payment, you will know that their intentions are not good. Even if their intentions are good at the beginning of the agreement, if later on they experience financial challenges, there is nothing to tie them down to the property. They will have nothing to lose—they don't even have the fear of damaging their credit. Their credit is damaged anyway and they will simply walk away from the lease-to-own agreement. However, if they have some of their hard-earned money invested in your property, they will think twice about abandoning it. If they refuse to give you a deposit as down payment, move on, find someone else.

Lease-to-own experiences

Another important point that I would like to share with you is that by nature we try to be nice to people, and many times this natural goodness gets us into trouble. I have had a few painful experiences with lease agreements where I felt sorry for the people because they had small children and I wanted to help them. I did not insist on a down payment deposit and in the course of the agreement, they just walked away from the lease-to-own agreement. They left behind a damaged and neglected property that cost me a few thousand dollars to repair. From my experience, I have learned and now realize that you must look after your own best interest. If you don't, no one else will.

The second painful lesson I have learned was *not* to allow the future homebuyer into the property without receiving the down payment deposit upfront. In this example, we agreed that they would move in with their family and in two weeks, they would give me a down payment deposit. You can imagine what happened. Two weeks later, they told me a tall story that he did not have any money to give me for the down payment deposit. By this time, he had moved into the house and because they had not violated the rental agreement, I could not evict them without a reason. It took me a year before I could get him out of the house. Learn from my painful experience; insist on a down payment deposit before you hand over the keys to your property.

In future dealings, I insist on obtaining a minimum of five percent of the future purchase price as mentioned earlier. However, if the tenants can only produce three or four percent up front, it may be worth considering. In a case like this, the tenants must agree to give you additional cash on top of the rent every month until you have received the full deposit amount of at least five percent. To do this you will need to calculate the total five percent deposit for the down payment of the future purchase price, subtract the amount of money that they are giving you and divide this amount by the amount of months in the lease-to-own agreement.

Let's continue with this example. Suppose that in your area a full three-bedroom, two-bathroom property is renting for $1,000.00.

Since you are giving them the right to purchase your house in the future, you should increase the rent amount by one or two hundred dollars per month, creating a larger cash flow for you. If they do not agree to these terms, look for another potential tenant. Remember that you are giving them a second chance to own a home when the bank is not even willing to consider giving them a loan.

An additional benefit to this strategy is that you will not have to deal with the tenants calling you at three in the morning because the toilet is flooded. As the future homeowners, they will need to take care of the maintenance of the property. You will have specified this in the lease-to-own contract by stating something like, "you as the future homeowner are responsible for all maintenance of the property." You will find that in most cases the new homeowner likes this clause because it gives them a sense of ownership. They begin to see the property as their own home, they will take care of it and they will be very grateful to you for giving them a second chance to own a home.

Now you have learned how to negotiate with the bank to get out of an upside down position into a break-even position. From the break-even position, you turned it around and made it a profitable position. In addition, you have saved your credit by getting out of a foreclosure situation, you have learned a great deal on how to solve problems, and you are walking away with cash in your pocket. Great!

Chapter 7
Preparing Mentally to Defend Your Home

IF YOU HAVE followed my instructions in the previous chapters, you should be ready to go to battle with the bank. By now, you should have gathered all the relevant information, including:

- Legal advice from a professional real estate lawyer

- A completed income and expense sheet detailing every aspect of your current financial condition

- Formulated a number of strategies to present to the bank collection agent and,

- Created a plan for defending your home.

Do you feel ready to defend your home? Even though you are as prepared as you will ever be, most likely you are experiencing a great deal of anxiety right now, and even though you have done all the preparation work up to this point, you have not paid any attention to the most important piece of the puzzle. That is *you*.

You are the most important part in this whole process, and your mental preparation will have the greatest influence on the outcome. All the information that you have gathered to this point will be rendered useless if you are not mentally prepared to defend your home. It all comes down to you as a person. Your success or failure will be determined by the actions you take. If you are not mentally prepared, you will fail to take any action. Perhaps you have heard professional athletes make the following comment "it is 90 percent mental." Whatever the percentage may be, if you fail to prepare yourself mentally for the challenges that lay ahead, you will procrastinate in doing the things that need to be done in a timely manner. It will hinder you from taking any type of action; eventually you will fail in your attempt to defend your home because you will run out of time. In your case, time is working against you.

The purpose of this chapter is to help you mentally prepare to face the decisive moment. The moment when you will have to pick up the phone, make the call, and arrange a face to face meeting with your bank collection agent. Yes, you must make an appointment to speak with the very same person that is making your life miserable. The very same person that has been calling you day and night demanding money that you do not have. This is not going to be easy, how can you muster up enough courage to do it? I know that it is going to be a very difficult step. I know how you feel; I have been there. I know you are afraid. However, this is something that no one else can do for you. You will have to be mentally prepared in order to amass the strength to pick up the phone and make that call. I hope that this chapter will inspire you and encourage you to do what you must do.

Make the decision to defend your home

It all starts in your mind. Make a firm and committed decision to defend your home. Regardless of the obstacles, challenges, and objections, just by making the decision to defend your home, will greatly improve your chances of success. A firm decision is not an idle wish, a whim, or the attitude of "I will give it a try to see what happens." The type of commitment you must make is one where you will defend your home against all odds, where you will not take "NO" for an answer. You will fight to protect what belongs to you, even if your life depends on it, and in reality, your financial life *does*.

Let me tell you a story to illustrate what I mean by making a committed decision. Perhaps you saw this report on the news quite a few years ago.

It is the story of a young family camping in the foothills of the Rocky Mountains. They wanted to be away from all the noise of a busy campground, so they selected a nice isolated spot away from everyone.

After they got up in the morning and while the wife was preparing breakfast, her husband decided to go for a walk with his few-month-old baby strapped to his back in a backpack baby carrier. His wife decided to cook bacon and eggs that morning. As you all know, when you cook bacon, you can smell it miles away. There are many bears in this part of the country and the bear could smell the bacon. The husband was returning from his walk, and as he was approaching their camp spot, a bear attacked him from behind. The bear grabbed the baby that was strapped to his back and in this situation he could not turn around to defend the baby or himself.

His wife, who was a short distance away when the bear attacked them, could hear her baby crying. She looked up towards her family and she could see the hopeless situation both her baby and her husband were in. She needed to make a decision quickly. She could run away and hide in her car and wait for the bear to consume her family or take a stand and fight against the bear with her bare hands and defend her family. In a split second, she reasoned that she could run away from the scene and allow the bear to devour her family. However, if she did run away, she would live with the regret of abandoning her family for the rest of her life. What kind of life would that be? She decided that the price was a price she was not willing to pay. She refused to live with the "what if" questions that usually come after a difficult decision is made. At that very moment she made a firm and committed decision—she was going to take a stand and fight the bear; she was going to defend her family even at the cost of her life.

Bears are very powerful animals, and no one in their right mind would go after a bear with bare hands. It did not matter to her that the bear was many times bigger, heavier, and faster than she was. It did not matter to her that the claws of a bear can cut off the head of a large moose in a single swipe. None of those things mattered to her. In fact, she did not even consider them. She had made a firm and committed decision. She was going to defend her family, regardless of the consequences.

In the heat of the moment, she never considered her own safety. The only thing that mattered to her was to save her family. She had no weapons to fight off the bear, and even if she did, she did not have the time to get them. Time was a commodity that she did not possess. Therefore, she grabbed the only thing that was at hand—her frying pan and she went after the bear. She ran to where the attack was taking place and she started to hit the bear over its head with the frying pan. She hit that bear with all her might, repeatedly until the bear let go of her baby and when the bear turned against her, she kept hitting that bear until the bear ran away. There are deep scars left in all of them, but she had accomplished a feat that most experts would label impossible. She made a firm, unwavering decision. She was going to defend her family even at the cost of her life and she succeeded.

This story illustrates the type of commitment that you will need to make in order to be successful in defending your home and it all starts by making a decision to do it. Before you take a single step forward, you must make the committed and unwavering decision to stand and fight for what is yours. You cannot sit idle as a spectator watching someone take away the roof over your family's head. You should not allow anyone to come and kick you out of your own home without a fight, and if you end up losing your home, you will have the peace of mind that you did everything you could to defend your home. You will live your life without regret.

Now I would like to ask you to do something. Please get up and go stand in front of the mirror, look intently into the eyes of the reflection in the mirror and while you are staring into those eyes say this statement out loud, "I am going to defend my home. I am not going to allow anyone to take away my home. I will not go down without a fight. I am going to defend my property no matter what."

This is the type of committed, unwavering decision that you will need to make, in order to be successful in defending your home. Anything less than this level of commitment will only produce results that may not be what you set out to accomplish. A halfhearted attempt will only produce a halfhearted result. I once heard someone say, *"Trying is failing with honors"* and I tend to agree with this statement. I will tell you this much, if your mindset is to try to defend your home, you will most likely fail in your attempt. You must *do*! In order to attain success, you must make a committed, unwavering decision to defend your home, regardless of the obstacles and objections. Once you make up your mind to stand and defend what belongs to you, you will be motivated to move into action and you will do the things that must be done in order to save the roof over your head.

Work out a plan

Now that you have made a firm unwavering decision to defend your home, you must work out a plan of action. At this point, you need to revisit the information that you've gathered as outlined in all the previous chapters.

I am going to assume that you have done all your homework and followed my instructions as suggested. You will require this information in order to prepare a proper defense plan. If you've failed to follow my instructions and decided to skip a few steps, I would like to encourage you to go back and obtain the information previously suggested. It is of vital importance that you obtain this information before we move forward. You should give this step the highest level of priority.

How will you be able to work out a plan to solve your problem, when you don't have all the facts in front of you? It would be like deciding to take a road trip from Toronto, Canada to Washington, DC in a 24-hour time frame without a map or GPS. What is the chance of you making a successful trip in the allotted time? If you are foolish enough to take your chances and make the trip anyway, after 24 hours of driving you will arrive somewhere, but you will most likely not be in the place where you had set as the destination.

I can't stress enough the importance of gathering all the information. If you have not done it yet, I strongly encourage you to stop. Do not take any further steps until you do so. Any steps that you take without accurate information, will most likely lead you in the wrong direction, it will be a waste of time, and in your case, time is a commodity that you do not possess. Once you have the accurate information, you will be able to sit down and analyze the facts in order to consider your options and work out a plan of action.

Create an action item list

One of the first things that I suggested earlier in this book was to obtain legal advice. I hope you followed my suggestion. Only a real estate lawyer can give you accurate information on how the foreclosure process works in your area. If you have not done so, this should be the first item on your list.

As you go through the gathered information, you will need to create an action plan. In this plan, you will list all the action items in priority sequence with specific dates as to when they must be accomplished. This checklist needs a separate column added for completion dates listed. You must add dates to each item. Each item is time sensitive and failure to complete the task on time will create additional problems for you.

Every action plan will be different for every individual situation. For example, if you are one or two months late with your mortgage payment and you have not been served with the **"Petition to Foreclose"** (the lender's formal notice that they are asking the court to help them get back the money they loaned you), the first thing on your action item list should be to call the bank. Explain your situation and say that you will present them with a solution within two weeks. If you fail to contact the bank, the bank will start the court procedure and once the court and lawyers are involve, it becomes more expensive for you. Now you not only have to pay for your late payments and fees, you also will have to compensate the bank for the court filing fees and pay for their lawyer who prepared the documents that were filed in court.

However, if you already have received the **"Petition to Foreclose"** notice and you have never bothered to open the letter and you have been sitting on it for two weeks, the first action item should be to file a **"Response to the Petition to Foreclose"** with the real estate court. In most cases, you have 21 days to file a response from the day that you were served. If you have been sitting on it for two weeks, you only have one week to complete this. If you fail to file a response within 21 days of being served, you have forfeited your rights as a homeowner and the foreclosure procedure will proceed without you. You will no longer be able to defend yourself in the court of law.

What if you never bothered to open the mail and you were served two months ago? This means that you have lost the opportunity to file a **"Response to the Petition to Foreclose."** In most cases, there is the **"Right of Redemption."** This means that even after you have lost your house to the foreclosure proceedings, the **"Right of Redemption"** laws allow the original homeowner to reclaim their house. The **"Right of Redemption"** laws are complicated and vary from state to state, or from province to province. Thus, it is difficult to make a general statement. If your situation is such that the foreclosure procedure is well on its way, consulting a real estate lawyer should be a priority on your list.

Another important point to consider is the reason why you are not able to make your mortgage payments. Is it due to layoff, illness, divorce, etc.? Is your financial situation permanent or temporary? Is it long-term or short-term? Your answer to these questions should guide the actions you take to solve this problem.

The importance of these steps is that when you speak with the bank collection agent, you will be able to show them a plan on how you intend to resolve your financial challenges. If you show the lending officer a workable plan of action, and a well thought out solution, the lending officer will not only be impressed with you, but they will be more willing to help you and work with you. Remember, the bank does not want to take your home away; all they want is for you to keep making your regular mortgage payments.

Overcoming obstacles and objections

As part of your mental preparation, it is wise to include a list of potential obstacles that you will encounter as you prepare to defend your home. Furthermore, you will face objections and rejections and in some cases, they may even laugh at your suggestions. You must be prepared for any eventuality of this nature, and you need to plan on how you will respond to these objections.

To help you out, here is an example of a potential obstacle that you may encounter. If you have missed your mortgage payment there must be a good reason, and I will assume that there is not much money in your bank account or in your pocket at this point in time. The last thing you need is to spend money on lawyers—money that you don't have.

I suggested many times throughout this book that you should get legal advice from a professional real estate lawyer. If you have never used the services of a lawyer before, you are about to find out how expensive these services are. That is not all; most, if not all law firms, require a retainer. A retainer is a sum of money that you must give the law firm in advance, before they agree to talk to you to see if your case has any merit. This retainer can range from a few hundred dollars to a few thousand dollars, depending on the gravity of the case. Handing over this money may present a big challenge for you at this time. In addition, if you do not end up using their services, you most likely will not get your money back. In my experience, they always find a reason to keep your money.

How are you going to overcome this challenge? How are you going to come up with the money to obtain the information you need? You may want to talk to a family member or a friend and ask if they can lend you the money as one possible solution to this problem. Another option may be to call your local legal aid agency and ask them what the requirements are to qualify for legal aid services in a foreclosure situation. This may solve that obstacle. I hope that you can appreciate the fact that I am not trying to find a solution to every obstacle that you will encounter. I am only trying to illustrate how to approach the problems in order for you to find a way around these obstacles.

As you prepare yourself mentally on how to approach the bank collection agent and present them with different options, I can guarantee you will face many objections to your ideas. You will not only receive objections but you must be prepared to receive rejections as well. You must be mentally prepared for this. You must be prepared to hear the word "NO" as an answer and many times they will even laugh at your proposal or the requests that you are making.

Do not let that bother you; keep in mind that you are dealing with a bank collection agent. They have been trained to push your buttons, to play with your emotions and to push you to the limit in order to compel you to make up those late payments. They are trained professionals that do this every day. They know what to say, what specific words to use, and how to say them by using the right intonation to have maximum impact on your emotions. Do not be fooled into believing that this is going to be a walk in the park. It is going to be a battle, you must be prepared both mentally, and emotionally when you go out to meet them.

The job of the bank collection agent is to scare you into making up the late mortgage payments. The truth is that foreclosure is the only legal resource that they have at their disposal to recover their money and as we covered before, the foreclosure process is the last measure they want to use. Therefore, the next best tool is the scare tactics. They will threaten, raise their voice, and throw papers up in the air. They will do and say anything just to scare you into making the late mortgage payments; they don't have any other recourse.

If, in fact, the case goes through foreclosure, they could do the things that they are threatening you with like putting a judgment on you and suing you for mortgage deficiency. However, if, after the fact, your situation is such that you have to declare bankruptcy, they will not be able to recover any of their losses. Sometimes they will go as far as to make you believe that they don't care if your children don't have anything to eat. To them, making up the late payments should be your highest priority above all other things.

As you go through the process of mentally preparing to face the bank collection agent, keep in mind that these people that are making your life miserable, to say the least, are also human beings with problems similar to yours and mine. At some point in time in the meeting, the bank collection agent will begin to consider the reality of the situation and become aware that he/she is not making much headway collecting the late mortgage payments from you. At the same time, hopefully sooner rather than later, he will consider the ever-increasing number of foreclosed properties being assigned to him on a weekly basis and will conclude that helping you is in his best interest.

Furthermore, their job security may be at risk. If the lending officer is not producing results, upper management will have to take drastic measures and appoint someone more experienced, forceful, and successful in the mortgage collection department. His job security depends on results and if the lending officer does not produce results, he will be out of a job.

When you have this insight, you must be prepared to appeal to their human side. Now you know that he is just as fearful as you are. He is afraid of losing his job as well, especially if he appears to be inadequate in producing results. In fact, he could find himself in the same predicament in a few short months if he is not able to complete his job effectively. If he is not able to scare you into making the late mortgage payments and you have all the evidence as to why you cannot make the payments, he may be more flexible and possibly consider your proposal. Be prepared to play the human card, keep it in your back pocket, and use it as a last resort. If all else fails, play this card. For you to be effective in appealing to their conscience, you need to prepare beforehand what you will say and how to say it for maximum effectiveness.

Also, decide ahead of time the minimum result you are willing to accept after meeting with the lending officer. If you are not able to get what you want during the first encounter, do not be afraid to walk away. The lending officer may try to force you to make a commitment that you will not be able to honor later on. When he counters your proposal, you must tell him that you are not willing to accept those terms now. Ask for a few days to consider the proposal. This response will provide you with the opportunity to leave his office and consider the counterproposal. It will also allow you time to reflect and come up with an alternate counterproposal that is more agreeable for you and the bank.

As you prepare a proposal, you must give careful consideration to what objections they may raise. Spend some time considering the bank's potential reaction to your proposal and what your response will be. As you consider their response, ask yourself these three simple questions:

1. What would be the worst thing that they can say to me?

2. What would be the best thing that they can say to me?

3. What is the most likely thing that they will say to me?

Consider all possible objections and reactions and prepare a response for each scenario. Furthermore, if the first proposal is completely rejected, have a second proposal in hand to present to them. To be successful in preparing your responses, you need to put yourself in their shoes. You need to see things from their point of view. What is it that the bank really wants? The obvious answer is that they want their money back. Well, they cannot have it all back, but if they are willing to work with you, they will be able to get most of it back. As you go through this exercise, you will be able to respond to their objections in an intelligent way and find a solution that is acceptable and fair to all parties involved.

Be clear, draw a line and determine what the minimum result is that you are willing to accept—make this decision before you talk to them. You cannot cross that line. If you do cross it, you will fall back into financial challenges, and that is what you are trying to avoid. You do not want to be speaking with the bank collection agent every three or four months because you were not able to keep the previous agreement. As I mentioned before, do not be afraid to walk away from the negotiating table, BUT always leave the door open for further negotiation. If you have made some headway in the right direction, ask the lending agent to put it in writing. This will become the basis to start the next round of negotiations.

The more time you spend preparing yourself mentally for any obstacles, objections, and rejections, the better chance you have of getting the desired result. When you are prepared to take "**no**" for an answer, you will know exactly how to respond to every objection that they throw at you. The better prepared you are, the more confident you will be when the time comes to face the bank lending officer.

Three possible outcomes

There will be three possible outcomes at the end of the negotiations with the bank lending officer and by having a clear goal in mind, you will be able to determine if you have won, lost or have come out with a draw. You must be absolutely clear as to what it is that you want as the outcome, what your objective is. If you fail to have a clear goal in mind, it will be impossible to measure with any degree of certainty the result of your success.

Furthermore, you must be absolutely clear as to what each one of these three possible outcomes means to you. As an example, what does a win mean to you in an upside down or underwater situation? Bringing your mortgage balance to a break-even position, would be a huge win for most people in this situation. However, you need to consider whether or not that is good enough for you.

For the sake of argument, let's say that the fair market value of the property is $200,000 and the balance on the mortgage is $300,000. That means that you are $100,000 underwater. Your mortgage interest is a five percent fixed rate for 25 years and you are three months behind on your payment with a mortgage payment of $1,750.00 monthly. What would you consider a win in this example? The bank agrees to forgive $100,000 of the mortgage amount to bring it in line with the fair market value of the property? The bank also agrees to forgive your late mortgage payments and waives off all late fees? The bank agrees to lower their interest rate on the new loan amount to three percent fixed rate for 25 years? This would lower your mortgage payment to $950.00 per month and the only requirement stipulated by the bank is that you make your payments on time every month. This would be the best outcome. This would be considered a *huge* win, and it is not a far-fetched thought. This could happen in the current real estate market conditions. However, the real outcome may be somewhere in between. If you can accomplish some of the points listed above and if you can live with the new agreement with the bank, then this would be considered a win situation for you and for the bank. Even if after much negotiation, you only accomplished the stopping of the foreclosure procedure. As a result, you save your credit record and arrange an agreement to stay in your home with much lower monthly payments; this is also considered a win. You need to decide beforehand what would be the minimum result that you would consider in order for you to call it a win.

Let's say that you have identified five concessions that the bank must make to make it a 100 percent success. If you get four out of five items, will you consider it a win? Or will you be arguing for the last item and feel really sad that you did not get it all? Chances are quite high that you will not get them all, but you can get most of them. You must identify the items that are of greatest importance to you so that you will emphasize them during the negotiation meeting.

Before you go to see the bank collection agent, you need to prepare a list of items that are important to you as part of the negotiation and list them in priority sequence. For example, item one should be a complete forgiveness of the late mortgage payments or, at the very least, a monthly repayment schedule. Another item may be (especially if you are in an underwater situation) to ask the bank to forgive the difference between the mortgage balance and the fair market value of the property and as a result, you will decrease your monthly payments. You must identify every point of importance and bring it up for negotiation. You must have a list of all these items before you go to speak to them. Try, to the best of your ability, to negotiate the important items first. Focusing on the important items first will take care of the small items by default. For example, monthly payments will be taken care of as a result of negotiating the bigger items like interest rates.

You will need to have a clear picture in your mind as to what a win for you will look like. Remember to *"ask for what you want and you will be surprised to see what people will do for you when you ask."*

What would you consider a loss? If the bank's lending officer refuses to budge on any of the key elements, it means that he does not see the need to forgive any portion of the mortgage loan amount, or even consider the possibility of making a repayment arrangement for the late mortgage payments or fees. In addition, he refuses to lower the interest rate and insists on going forward with the foreclosure procedure. In such a case, it will be a loss for you and the bank and as mentioned earlier, if the bank is unwilling to forgive the difference between the fair market value of the property and the mortgage balance, the bank is heading towards a bigger loss by refusing to negotiate with you. Once they include all of the court fees, realtor fees, legal fees and other holding costs until the property sells, the bank's losses will be higher than if it were willing to work with you.

Therefore, it is your responsibility to educate the bank collection agent with the facts that you have collected and remind them of the current real estate market condition. It will be part of your negotiation strategy to enlighten the bank collection agent as to how much more the bank will lose by refusing to help you and to work with you to find a solution beneficial to both parties. By presenting the bank with hard evidence on the reality of the market condition, the collection agent must be flexible to accommodate at least some, if not all, of your requests. By refusing to work with you as a homeowner and many other homeowners that will come after you, the banks are threatening their very existence as lending institutions.

What would you consider a draw? In this case, the bank is flexible enough to agree to some of your demands and it is something you can live with. In this case, the bank is willing to stop the foreclosure procedure by forgiving all your late mortgage payments and fees. In addition, the bank will forgive only half ($50,000) of the underwater amount, but they are unwilling to lower the five percent interest rate. Your new mortgage payment will be $1461.00, which is still better than the original situation. If you can live with that arrangement then that may be the best that you can do.

If you are not fully satisfied with the outcome of the negotiation, you do not have to accept it; you may want to ask the bank for a `time-out' to consider further options. During the 'time-out', give further consideration to the solutions presented during the negotiation phase. You may have to come up with different ideas that will produce a better outcome, one that will meet your needs and at the same time satisfy the requirements of the bank. Remember: You do not have to agree to the first thing that the bank offers you; they have as much to lose as you do. You may have to remind the bank collection agent of this fact more than once during the negotiation stage. It will help keep him from trying to overpower you. You must treat this as a business negotiation that requires the cooperation of both parties to make it acceptable and profitable for all involved.

Chapter 8
Prepare Yourself Emotionally

THERE IS ONE more vital aspect that we must address prior to moving forward with contacting your bank collection agent. Even before you make the call to set up an appointment to meet him in person, you must deal with the matter of your emotions.

In the previous chapter, we covered the importance of being mentally prepared. However, being mentally prepared for the challenge ahead may not be enough. Your emotions also play a very important role. It is the engine that moves your body into action and if you are experiencing the wrath of a foreclosure proceeding, and find yourself in peril of losing your home, you must be experiencing a great deal of anger, fear, and anxiety at this moment.

The first negative emotion that you may experience under these types of circumstances is anger, and many times the anger that is bottled up inside of us bubbles up and explodes. When this happens, innocent bystanders suffer the consequences. Unfortunately, more often than not, we take out this anger on our loved ones, the ones closest to us, mainly our spouse, or our children.

Before you explode or direct your anger at someone, consider that your close family members are as scared as you are. You don't need to take out your frustrations on them. It is not their fault that you are where you are financially. They can see the fear on your face, they can sense it, and someone has to be the mature adult in the family. What they want and need to hear from you at this moment is a word of encouragement like *"Everything is going to be o.k."*

I would like to keep reminding you to repeat these six simple words to your family members: *"Everything is going to be o.k."* You really have no idea of the positive impact that those simple words have on a troubled heart.

In addition to anger, we also need to deal with two other negative emotions and that is fear and anxiety. One of the main causes of fear and anxiety is *lack of knowledge.* Not knowing what is ahead will cause us to become afraid. However, by now, you should have gathered all the information that was suggested throughout the previous chapters and you are now prepared to face the bank collection agent. Furthermore, you have taken some steps to be mentally prepared for the occasion. But it seems as though your logical mind (where information is stored) does not communicate that information to your emotional mind (where your feelings are stored). Although you have all this information in your head, you may still be experiencing a great deal of fear and anxiety at this moment. Sometimes it gets to the point where you feel sick and experience symptoms of depression.

Therefore, before you set your defense plan in motion, you must first consider your emotions. You need to find out where you are emotionally in order to be able to deal with a banker in the proper manner. Unfortunately, for most families experiencing the foreclosure phenomenon, their emotions are in a state of chaos. Family members are angry, nervous, frustrated, and scared. All of this creates a tense and unpleasant family life.

They are experiencing what I call *'emotional bankruptcy'* If this is your case, you must stop and consider the root cause of the situation and stop blaming everyone and everything for your current situation. Things happen to good and bad people for many reasons: poor judgment, lack of foresight, or a simple miscalculation. These types of things can happen to anyone at any given time. Please stop blaming others or yourself; learn from this experience and move on.

The topic of dealing with your emotions is very critical when dealing with a foreclosure situation. Under the circumstances, most if not all, of the emotions that you are experiencing at this moment are all negative in nature and none of these emotions will help you to get out of the hole that you are in. You cannot expect positive results by indulging in negative emotions. Furthermore, all of the negative emotions you are experiencing are not helping you come up with any good ideas to solve the problem. In fact, they do quite the opposite: these negative emotions cloud your ability to reason and paralyze you from taking action.

Even though it may seem as though your world has been turned upside down and at this very moment you may be experiencing a number of negative emotions, I would like to remind you of the phrase that my wife used to tell me when we were going through our own foreclosure process: **"Everything is going to be o.k."**

Losing your home to foreclosure is a traumatic experience and it will take some time to heal the emotional wounds left by it. However, I would like to encourage you by telling you that regardless of how you feel at the moment, it is not the end of the world. Life goes on even after you have lost your home if it must come to that. You and your family will not cease to exist because of it.

You will survive and when the dust settles you will be much wiser and emotionally stronger. Little bumps in the road like the impending danger of losing your home will never shake you again. One day you will look back and laugh at your current situation and perhaps you may be saying to yourself, I wish I could believe you. Believe me, I have been there, I have gone through the whole process. I know that it was not the most memorable time in my life and the experience was very unpleasant. I survived and now I am here twenty years later, writing a book to offer help to those who are currently experiencing this foreclosure nightmare.

Overcoming anger

Many years ago, I was sharing an office with a retired corporate lawyer. After spending many hours talking to him, we got to know each other very well. Through all of our conversations, I learned many valuable lessons from his personal life experiences.

On one occasion, I got a phone call informing me that one of my children had done something that I had specifically told her not to do before going to work that morning. Needless to say, when I heard what she had done I immediately reacted with an outburst of anger. I was furious!

The lawyer friend of mine looked at me and asked me in a calm tone of voice, "Problems at home?" Yes, I responded, and I started to tell him what my daughter had done and I ended the sentence with "she makes me so angry." He calmly asked me another question. He asked, "What are you afraid of?"

I looked at him as though he did not hear what I had said previously. I was not afraid, I was angry. I asked him, "Did you hear what I just told you? I am not afraid, I am angry," and I turned around to continue working on my computer.

He called my attention again and he repeated the question, "What are you afraid of?" He proceeded with a calm voice to tell me that in his experience, whenever he sees that someone is very angry, he sees someone who is very afraid. At that time, his statement did not help me change my state of mind. Before I could interject, he continued and said, "If you can figure out what is making you afraid and you learn to deal with that fear, your anger will go away."

At that moment in time, I did not give much thought to that statement, but over the years I have discovered that the advice my lawyer friend gave me is invaluable. It is a very useful tool I still use in my life to deal with outbursts of anger whenever they arise. Every time something happens to anger me, I remember to take one step back and consider the root of my anger. More often than not, I identity that fear is the root cause. Once I identify the cause, I can move on to deal with the problem or situation in a proper way.

Give this statement some consideration and try to incorporate it into your day-to-day life. When something happens, take one step back and consider what is making you afraid. Once the fear has been identified, you can deal with it in a more composed manner and you will be able to remove the anger that is inhibiting your thought process from your emotions.

Overcoming fear and anxiety

Fear and anxiety is where it all begins. Once you start to receive threatening phone calls and letters in the mail, fear begins to take hold of your emotions and as you allow fear to settle in, it progresses into anxiety. If you let anxiety control your emotions, it will progress into depression and eventually physical or emotional disease. What is fear? If you look up the term in the dictionary, it will tell you that "fear is a distressing emotion aroused by impending danger, evil, pain, etc. whether the threat is real or imagined." Fear is a negative emotion that does not originate with fear itself; the origin of fear is worry.

For example, when you have been laid off from your job, and there is not much money in the bank, you begin to worry about your finances. How are you going to make ends meet? How are you going to feed your family? How are you going to pay the bills? You begin to consider how bad the reality of your financial situation is and you begin to worry. Now to worsen the situation you begin to receive letters from your creditors demanding payment, and disconnection notices from your utility company and to top it all off, you begin to receive abusive and threatening calls from collection agencies. All of these calls and/or letters serve as a permanent reminder of the poor condition of your financial situation. It seems to be the perfect storm, and there you are with your family trying to navigate through this financial mess in your little rubber dingy.

Needless to say, such a situation would make anyone worry and even afraid. However, as I mentioned before, fear is a negative emotion and the continuous calling from the collection agencies and creditors reminding you that you owe them money and that they want that money now, only injects even more fear into your very being. It is not helping you alleviate any emotional distress. The constant calls do nothing positive to help you with your emotions and consequently nothing good can come of it. If you allow fear to take hold of your emotions, it will only make matters worse. You may be asking yourself, how can it get any worse? If you let fear get ahold of your emotions and if you live in fear for a prolonged period of time it will produce anxiety, anxiety will produce depression and in many cases anxiety produces disease, which affects your physical body and may even lead to death.

There are many people today suffering from depression and the best that the medical doctors can do is to numb their system by drugging them with Valium. However, Valium will never solve your problem. You need to go back to the root cause of the problem. Consider what is making you angry and find out the fear that is associated with that anger. Deal with that fear by getting the truth out of the situation and once you learn the truth, the truth will set you free, and release you from your anxiety.

Everything in the universe vibrates and there are positive and negative vibrations. We as part of this universe are affected by it. Consider music as an example, music is one form of vibration. Some types of music make you feel good, other types of music make you feel sad, and under the right conditions may even make you cry. There is also the type of music that you cannot tolerate. Music is a type of vibration that influences the way you feel, and sometimes music has such a strong influence on us that it causes our entire body to move to the beat in rhythm with its vibrations. It has nothing to do with the lyrics of the song; it is the beat of the music, the rhythm, the vibration, that directly affects us. Let me prove it to you. Have you ever seen a one-year-old child listen to music that is playing in the background? After a short time, the child begins to move to the beat of the music. They don't have the ability yet to understand the lyrics, but the vibrations prompt this little child to move along to the beat.

As mentioned earlier, fear is a negative destructive emotion that produces a negative vibration. When you find yourself under the influence of a negative emotion, you can only expect to receive more emotions that have the same vibration frequency. In other words, because you are in harmony with a negative emotion, you can only expect to attract yourself to people and situations that are in the same frequency or the same level of vibration.

Did you ever notice when you were going to school that all the smart kids were always together, the kids who smoked were always together, the troublemakers were always together, etc. Have you ever considered why? Simply, they were in harmony with one another. They are at the same level of vibration; they feel comfortable with one another.

Until you are able to remove anger, worry, and anxiety, you will only attract more things that will cause you to experience more worries and fears. Have you ever noticed that when you get up in the morning and something goes wrong at the start of the day, everything seems to go wrong for the rest of the day? Moreover, when something good happens at the start of the day, the whole day seems to go that way? It has everything to do with the level of vibration that you are in. Until you are able to move out of the current level of negative vibration, you can only expect to receive more people, events and circumstances that are in harmony with your current level of vibration.

My hope is that you will grasp this concept. Now, how do you move out of the vibration that you are in? The best way is to focus on the solution to the problem and not on the problem itself. If all of your attention is focused on the problem, and based on the law of vibration, you will only attract more problems. However, if you dedicate all of your attention on finding a solution, ideas will begin to come to you naturally.

Problems and solutions are at opposite ends of the spectrum. When you are concentrating on the problem, you can't see the solution and when you are focusing on the solution, you can't see the problem. By focusing your conscious attention on the solution, you will move out of the negative vibration and move into a positive vibration. Once you are in a different level of vibration and hopefully a positive one, you will find a solution to your problem.

Overcoming blame and guilt

Blame and guilt are another set of negative emotions that we must consider further in order for you to move forward with a foreclosure defense plan.

Have you ever noticed that whenever we experience a negative event in our lives, by nature we always try to find someone to blame. It is human nature and perhaps you may have a good reason to blame someone or something—an act of nature, the economy, or an unforeseen catastrophic event that just landed in your lap. Blaming someone or something will never help you solve your current problem, even though you may be fully justified in blaming someone and perhaps you are an innocent victim of the circumstances.

Finding blame in yourself or someone else will not help you in any way and this is why. Each time you think about or repeat the same sad or traumatic incident to anyone that is willing to lend you an ear, of how someone else is to blame for all the problems in your life. As you repeat the story, you are re-living this negative experience mentally and emotionally. As we covered previously, your whole being moves into a negative vibration, and as a consequence, you keep attracting more negative experiences, for which you will need to keep finding someone or something to blame for your troubles. Perhaps repeating the story gives you a sense self-justification or perhaps what you are seeking is sympathy from other people. Regardless of the reason, the problem is not going to go away. You will never be able to achieve a positive result while indulging in a negative state of mind. Blaming someone, blaming yourself, or blaming something will not help you deal with the real issue, which is the foreclosure preceding. If you don't believe me, test it for yourself. See how much progress you make by blaming someone.

This is the test. Go to your bank and ask to speak to your bank manager or lending officer and start blaming everyone and everything for your financial problems. Try to justify not making the mortgage payments by blaming your spouse or your former boss for laying you off. You will soon learn that they really don't care who is to blame. Their only concerns are (1) how will you make up your late mortgage payments and (2) how will you pay back all of the money they lent you. They do not care why you can't make the mortgage payments on time or who is to blame. The bank's only concern is that you are late with the payments and they want their money now.

Blaming someone or something will never help you solve your problem because your mind can only concentrate on one item at a time. When your whole attention is dedicated exclusively on finding someone to blame you are not able to consider any possible solutions to your problem. How can you find a solution to the problem? When you are not thinking about a solution, your attention is focused *on* the problem.

While you are spending all of your valuable time playing the blame game, the foreclosure clock is ticking. If you do not take any countermeasures, you will end up losing your home for failing to take action. One of the main reasons why people end up losing their home to foreclosure is that they fail to take any action.

At some point in our lives, we must behave as mature, responsible adults and take full responsibility for our financial situations, whether we were directly or indirectly responsible for them. If you continue to indulge yourself in finding someone to blame, you will not be able to find a solution. Once you take responsibility for your financial situation, you will be able to move forward and find a solution.

The best thing to do is to avoid any thoughts or feelings of guilt and blame. As soon as your thoughts begin to drift into blaming someone, quickly discard those thoughts and start to consider solutions. It does not matter who is to blame; what matters now is that you are only considering thoughts that will solve your problem.

Guilt is another negative emotion that we have not covered yet. Guilt and blame are two emotions that are closely related. While blame is anger or resentment directed at someone else, guilt is anger or resentment directed at ourselves. In our own personal lives, we all have done things in the past that we are not proud of. In fact, we may have done some things that we are ashamed to admit. In many cases, our decisions have brought us catastrophic consequences as a result, and have had detrimental effects on our physical and emotional health, as well as on our finances.

Every time someone in our life circle makes a mistake (such as a loved one, family member, or a business partner) we form an opinion about the character of that person. When we make a mistake, we condemn ourselves and we form an opinion about our own character as well.

Have you ever heard comments like the ones below? Or maybe you are guilty of making the same comments yourself. Comments such as, "I am such an idiot," "Only a fool could do something so stupid," "That is why I make mistakes, because I am an idiot," or any variation of the above. Do you think that these types of comments about oneself will help improve your decision-making ability or stop you from making mistakes in the future? Do you think that such comments will help you make better decisions? I doubt it.

If you have made mistakes in the past and I am sure that you have, maybe it is time to let them go. Holding on to the memory of those mistakes is not doing anything positive for you. It is time to learn to forgive yourself. We all have made poor decisions or demonstrated poor judgment at some point in our lives. There is nothing that can be done about it. The only thing that can be done is to learn from that mistake and move on. There is no point on reliving the past. What is done is done.

Guilt is a powerful negative emotion and if you allow it to take hold of your emotions, it has the potential to lead you to harm your physical body. I remember once I was on vacation in Los Angeles with my family and as we were walking down the street, we encountered a man that was overcome by guilt and anger. As he was walking down the street, he was cursing and slapping himself for being so stupid. Perhaps you have heard of similar cases where people whip themselves, or in some cases commit suicide, because they have been overtaken with guilt and they would rather die than keep on living in their current situation.

Once you have identified guilt as one of the negative emotions controlling you, you must eradicate it immediately; do not let it take hold of you. It is like going to the movies and the movie turns out to be a really bad movie. Would you ever waste your time and money on going to see the same bad movie again? I am quite sure that you would refuse. However, when it comes to your life experiences, especially the bad life experiences, why do we find pleasure in revisiting them? Every time we experience guilt, it is like going to a live theater to relive that painful and traumatic experience. You are reliving the experience in full color on the screen in your mind. Do you see any profit in doing that? So, why do we do it? It is as if we get some sort of satisfaction in doing so, or we may have the wrong concept, thinking that by reliving the experience, we will find forgiveness if we truly express regret.

As mentioned before, by indulging in this type of negative emotion, you will only move into a negative level of vibration and consequently, it will attract you to experiences that are negative in nature. You must learn to forgive yourself; neither you nor I can change the past and it is time to let it go.

Overcoming shame

Shame is another negative and paralyzing emotion. This emotion is probably the most destructive in terms of finding a solution to your financial problems. It causes you to hide the problem from the people that may have the ability to help. Instead of seeking help from family and/or friends about the true condition of your finances, you hide it from them.

It is no secret that no one likes to talk about their personal financial situation, especially if the picture is not good. When we are experiencing financial challenges, we hide this information, even from our spouse, or in somecases especially from our spouse. It is considered a very private matter that should only be discussed if it is absolutely necessary. However, like all things, the truth eventually does come out. Once the truth comes out and your true financial status is exposed, it may be too late for any financial assistance that a family member and/or friend could have offered. By this, I am not suggesting that you should tell everyone you meet about your financial problems, but I am sure there are a handful of people in your life that you can entrust with your financial challenges. If you trust them enough, you may want to solicit financial assistance from them or, at the very least, they should be able to give you moral support. They may even be able to offer you an idea that may help you solve your financial problem.

This emotion has a paralyzing effect; it stops you from seeking help and from doing anything to solve the problem. Instead of spending time to find a solution to the problem, you are busy finding ways to hide the problem. The only thing on your mind is how to save face because you don't want anyone to know. While you are all caught up entertaining thoughts of "what will my friends and family think?" "How am I going to tell my spouse?" "How am I going to tell my parents?" We are paralyzed from taking any action and we go on pretending that everything is fine. All the while, the foreclosure clock is ticking and eventually that dreadful day arrives and your house is confiscated and you are forced to move out.

What your friends or family say or think of you should be the least of your worries. Yes, there a great deal of shame to admit that you have lost your house to a foreclosure, but it is what it is. You are not the first person to lose a home and most likely will not be the last. Bad things happen to good and bad people alike and unfortunately, you are no exception. There may be good reasons as to why they happened, or there may be poor reasons. Now looking back on my own experience, it would have been less shameful to ask for financial help from my family and friends than to have to admit that I lost my home to a foreclosure.

The choice is yours. Do you tolerate a little shame now by having to ask for help from your family and friends? Or do you have a bigger shame later when you have to admit that you lost your home to a foreclosure?

If you open up your financial problems to a friend or a family member, they may be able and willing to help you so that you can keep your home. One of the comments that we heard from our friends and family members after we lost our house was, "Why didn't you tell us about your financial problems? We could have helped you. We had some money in savings that we were not using that we could have lent you until your financial situation improved." We were so good at hiding our financial condition that no one had a clue that we were losing our home until it was too late. We, in fact, lost our house and ruined our credit over a few thousand dollars. There were people in our lives that cared for us. People that were willing and able to help us if we would have just opened our mouths and asked for help. Do not try to be a hero, get beyond shame, and ask for help; there is no pride in having to admit that you have lost your home in a fore-closure. There are people in your life that care for you and they are willing to help you if they know that you need help.

Please keep in mind that you have nothing to gain but a lot to lose by hiding your true financial situation. You know who your friends are, you know who in your family you can trust, and who has the ability to help you. Talk to them, seek help, get beyond shame and you may be happily surprised at the outcome.

We have covered a lot of material in this book so far, and I have given you many suggestions throughout the book. In addition, I have given you a few ideas on how to approach problems and how to find potential solutions for them. By now you should have a good number of ideas of your own on how to solve your foreclosure problem. However, the best ideas in the world will be rendered useless if you fail to implement them and neglect to take any action.

Chapter 9
Helpful Tips

I FEEL THAT there are a couple of items that you may or may not have given much thought to in the past. I feel that these tips will not only serve you well during your encounter with the bank collection agent, but serve you as a useful tool in your everyday life.

Dressing for the meeting

Quite often, men give very little consideration to the clothing we wear. Women have a lot more common sense than we do when it comes to selecting the clothing to wear for a particular occasion. Since we give very little thought to the matter of selecting the proper clothing to wear for a particular event, quite often we find ourselves either over- or under-dressed for the occasion, which causes us to feel uncomfortable during the entire event. Our attire affects our confidence, self-assurance and the way we feel.

Furthermore, you may have heard the saying that you only have one chance to make a good first impression. If this is true, you may not want to miss the opportunity to make a good first impression in any relevant event in your life.

I would like to insert a little disclaimer here since I am not a world expert in clothing coordination and I am only offering common sense suggestions on what to wear for the face-to-face appointment with the bank collection agent. My common sense suggestions do not come from me, they come from my wife and three daughters. They quite often tell me that a change of clothes is necessary.

For your upcoming meeting with the bank collection agent, you must give careful consideration to the matter of the clothing that you will wear. You do not want to give the wrong first impression and the clothing you wear speaks volumes about your person character. You must dress properly. Keep in mind the 'expression without is a re-flection of the person within.' In other words the clothing worn ex-presses the character of the person. I am not suggesting that the clothing you wear makes you as a person. As an example, if you dress like a doctor with a white garment and stethoscope, it will not make you a doctor. Alternatively, I would find it very difficult to believe that you would allow a person dressed in jeans and a muscle shirt to perform open-heart surgery on you.

For this very reason, you need to pay attention to the clothing that you wear for this occasion. You should dress in a dignified way, giv-ing careful consideration to the type of work that you do. For exam-ple, it would be inappropriate for an executive or a person working at a management level in a corporation to show up for the meeting with the bank collection agent wearing old jeans, a t-shirt with a huge col-orful beer logo on it and dirty running shoes. What kind of impres-sion will the bank collection agent have of a person dressed in such a way? It is highly unlikely that the bank collection agent will take any-thing this person says seriously. In this situation, a collared shirt and dress pants are more acceptable and a tie and suit if you deem it appropriate.

Another extreme example would be if a construction or factory worker showed up for this meeting wearing a three-piece silk suit or a tuxedo. This type of attire is not congruent with the type of work that he does. Therefore, you must choose clothing that is fitting with the type of work that you do and at the same time matches the occasion. In this situation, it is more appropriate to wear a pair of khakis and a nice dress shirt. Above all, please remember to polish your shoes. Your shoes speak volumes about your character, as well.

Keep in mind that when you applied for a mortgage with your bank, you gave them all your personal financial information. The bank collection agent knows everything there is to know about your personal finances. They even have access to your credit history. If you show up for this meeting wearing inappropriate clothing, it will likely take away your credibility and the credibility of your presentation.

When the time comes to make your presentation to the bank collection agent, you must convince them that you are a responsible, honest person and that you are serious and willing to do whatever it takes to save your home and at the same time help the bank minimize their loses, if the bank is willing to work with you. Your main purpose in this visit is to convince the bank collection agent that you are serious and the clothing that you wear will either help you or hurt you in accomplishing your mission.

Perish the thought that by dressing poorly or in rags you are going to get some sympathy or pity from the collection agent. Their main and only concern is how you are going to pay them back. However, if you show up dressed adequately for the occasion and present them with a well thought out plan, they will listen to what you have to say.

Body language

Imagine walking into a dark room and all you can hear is a dog barking at you, you don't know the size of the dog or the dog's intention because you can't see the dog. You really have no idea why the dog is barking at you. Is it because he sees you as a threat or is it because he is excited to see you and all he wants to do is play with you? However, if you could see the dog's tail wagging at you while it is barking, you would have a clear indication that the dog wants to play with you. What a different impression you would have of the situation if you could see the body language of the dog.

Due to the fact that animals can't communicate with us in a verbal form, we must rely on their body language to find out what they want to express to us. If you have ever owned a pet, you know what I am referring to. My grandmother used to say that you could always tell when the dog had been chewing on your sandals before you even saw the evidence.

You must be asking yourself, "What do dogs chewing on sandals have to do with being prepared to meet the bank collection agent?" We as humans do use our body to communicate with other humans and if you don't know the body language cues you will miss out on great opportunities. Unbelievably, people, as well as dogs, wag their tails when they want to play with you, but you need to acquire the basic knowledge of the human language to profit from it.

Body language is a fascinating topic, much too broad to cover in a single section of a book. I just want to give you enough information to prepare you for your encounter with the bank collection agent. Should you wish to pursue this topic further, I would strongly recommend an audio program by Peter Thomson called "The Best

Kept Secrets of Great Communicators" offered by Nightingale-Conant[4].

In this program, Peter explains that the majority of our conversations are non-verbal. Peter goes even further and breaks down our conversations into three main levels, what we say, how we say it and body language. What we say only accounts for seven percent of our conversation, how we say what we want to say, the intonations of your voice, account for 38 percent and your body language accounts for a staggering 55 percent of our conversations. Since body language accounts for such a high percentage of all of our conversations, perhaps it would be prudent to give it some consideration as you prepare yourself for the encounter with the bank collection agent.

As you walk into the office of the bank collection agent, reach out for the other person's hand and clasp it warmly, look directly into his/her eyes and say, "I am very glad to meet you." Practice making eye contact; failure to make eye contact says one or two things about you. It may say "I feel weak beside you," "I feel inferior to you," or "I am afraid of you." You say nothing good about yourself when you fail to make eye contact. Looking into the other person's eyes tells him/her "I am honest, I believe in what I am telling you and I am not afraid of you."

Pay close attention to what he/she says, but pay even more attention to his/her body language. You are looking for inconsistencies in what is being said and the banker's body language. For example, as you walk into the office, he/she welcomes you with a huge smile on his/her face and says, "Welcome, please come in and take a seat." The words are consistent with the body language. The other case will

---

[4] To obtain further information on how to purchase this program, refer to Appendix C or visit us at www.theforeclosurephenomenon.com

be that as you walk into the office, he/she welcomes you with a frown on his face and in a stern voice says, "Welcome, please come in and take a seat," as he points to a chair." In both examples, we used the same words. However, the intonation and the body language used in the second example gave you a completely different impression didn't it?

How can you use this knowledge? How can you use it to your advantage and move on with your presentation? First of all you will need to become familiar with the different body language gestures and their meaning. Secondly, as you move along with your proposal, you need to know beforehand how your proposal is being received by the collection agent. By paying close attention to his body language, you will know in advance, before he opens his mouth, whether your proposal is being accepted or rejected. If your proposal is being rejected, change your strategy, propose something else. Do not allow him to go as far as to verbally reject your proposal, for the simple fact that once he has rejected your proposal, he will have to defend that position, and it will become more difficult for you to get a positive result.

Therefore, if you know that your proposal is going to be rejected by accurately interpreting his body language, do not allow him to say no. Instead, keep talking and modify your proposal until you sense a change in his attitude. However, if you read his body language properly and he is showing a positive response to your proposal, stop talking and let him say yes, for the reason stated above. Once he gives you a yes answer, he will have to defend that position. I have seen this in numerous instances. The other person has accepted the proposal, idea, or suggestion and he is ready to say yes. However, you are not giving him the opportunity to give you the **"yes"** answer because you simply do not stop talking. Please, learn to read the body language signs and let him say *yes* to your proposal.

What are these body language gestures and signs and what do they mean? Again, I will emphasize that what I am giving you here is only a scratch on the surface of this topic, and what I am sharing with you is only what I think will be helpful to you in your presentation. For more information, I strongly encourage you to obtain the full version of "The Best-Kept Secrets of Great Communicators," by Peter Thomson, through Nightingale-Conant.

Furthermore, I would like to point out that we are talking about body language and that an individual body sign should not be taken in isolation. You shouldn't assume what the other person's response is going to be based on a single body sign.

• During a conversation, if the other person crosses his/her arms or assumes any other type of 'across the body' type of defensive posture, what does that mean? If the other person crosses his arms or legs, it usually means that he is not agreeing with what you are saying and he has adopted a defensive and negative position. Again, do not take a single body language gesture in isolation; crossed arms could mean that his hands are cold. However, if you see a frown on his face that is a strong indication that you are not making much headway. He is either not comfortable with you or with what you are saying and I would suggest that you change your body language, tone of voice, or the content of your presentation to a different strategy.

• During a conversation, if the other person leans toward you, what does that mean? If you are sitting next to each other or across from each other and the other person leans towards you with wide-open eyes, it could mean that the other person is in agreement with you and maybe he is excited to hear what you are saying or he feels comfortable being near you. He does not perceive you to be a threat and his wide-open eyes show that he is interested in what you are saying. However, if the other person leans away from you and his facial expression changes to a frown, he may even give you a suspicious look. I am sure that you can picture it. This could mean that the other person is not comfortable either with you, with the content of your presentation, or with your body language.

- If, during a conversation, the other person begins to speak and starts to pull down at his ears, looks sideways or pulls down the outside corner of his eyes, tugs sideways at the pocket on his shirt/suit, or covers his mouth, what does that mean? It is quite clear by all of these body language signs that this person is very uncomfortable with what is coming out of his mouth and it may be an indication that what he is saying is *not* true.

- If during the conversation the other person begins to brush imaginary flint from his clothing, what does it mean? He is simply telling you that he has had enough. He is bored and is no longer interested in paying attention to what you have to say. What should you do if this happens while in the midst of your presentation? If this is, in fact, the case, you must take action quickly and tell him something like this, "I know that you must be really busy and I don't want to take too much of your time. When is a better time to reschedule this appointment?" Once you get a new appointment time, ask him for feedback, probe him for additional information and specific aspects of the presentation that he is in agreement and disagreement with in order to create a better proposal for the next meeting.

- Imagine that you are sitting across the desk from another person. The other person pushes himself to the edge of the chair, and puts both of his hands on his knees as if he is about to get up. What does that mean? In addition, what should you do about it? This is another no-brainer body language sign. It is quite clear that he has had enough, the meeting is over, and he wants you out of his office. What should you do in such a situation? Especially when you are not finished making your point. If you are not finished making your point, the worst thing that you could do is to stand up and leave. If you have not gotten your point across yet, acknowledge their desire for you to leave by saying something like this while sitting down, "You must have other important matters to attend to. However, if you would just give me five more minutes of your time so that I can finish making my last point and make my proposal absolutely clear for you to consider, I would really appreciate it." You should immediately see a change in his body language. He will either, stand up and kick you out of his office, which would be highly unprofessional; Or he will sit back in his chair, adopting his original posture.

- If during a conversation the other person begins to rub his or her chin, what does that mean? In most cases, it simply means that the other person is giving careful consideration to what you are saying. If you have finished your presentation, do not interrupt him; give him enough time to consider your proposal. He may ask you additional questions to clarify matters and that is ok, as long as you have prepared yourself beforehand.

Eye movement offers another very important clue about how your presentation is being received. Pay close attention to a little red triangle located in the inner corner of the eye, close to the nose. That little red triangle along with other body language signs will give you the clearest indication of how your presentation is progressing.

When you are talking to another person and you can clearly see the other person's red triangle in the corner of his eyes, it is an indication that the other person feels comfortable with your presence and is in agreement with the content of the conversation. However, if he becomes uncomfortable or suspicious of what you are saying, the lower lids of his eyes will contract and move upwards, covering the little red triangle. It is almost like a squint. If you would like to try this yourself, stand in front of a mirror and try to see your own little red triangle. Try saying, "uhm, I am not sure about this information" while you are looking in the mirror. That is it, you got it.

When you can't see the other person's red triangle in the inner corner of his eyes, it is because he is either not comfortable with you or not comfortable with what you are saying. If you are in the middle of presenting your proposal to the bank collection agent, you need to figure out quickly what has made them uncomfortable. Is it you? Maybe your tone of voice, maybe your facial expression, or it may be *your* body language. If, in fact, it is you, you need to change the delivery of your presentation quickly. However, if it is the content of your proposal, you will need to make a modification to your proposal. Use this sign as a compass to guide you during the presentation. The trick is to be able to keep an eye on the red triangle without staring at the person to the point that he will feel uncomfortable.

How will you find out what has caused a change in his attitude? The simplest way would be to ask him an indirect question. As an example, you could ask something like, "How do you feel about my proposal thus far?" If it is the proposal that has caused the contraction in his attitude, he will tell you something and whatever he responds will give you an indication if it is the proposal or if it is you. Once you know which one it is, make the necessary corrections to appease him.

Because you are conducting the presentation in a hostile environment, to say the least, and you can't trust what the banker is saying to you, you must learn to read between the lines and the little red triangle at the corner of the eye. This will be of great help to you.

There is one simple rule for this body language sign, never ask for a "yes" answer if you can't see the red triangle in the inner corner of the other person's eye. I hope that from this moment on, you will start to practice looking at people's eyes as you converse with them. Paying attention to the little red triangle will serve you well in many aspects of your life. It will give you a clear indication of what the other person is thinking about when you are talking.

It is said that the only part of the brain that we can see is the eyes, and I tend to agree with that statement. Remember never to ask for a "yes" answer if you can't see the little red triangle in the other person's eyes[5].

We have covered a great deal of information in this chapter and my hope is that you will use the information presented to you. Hopefully you will get a positive result in your endeavor to defend your home. I really don't know what else you can do to be any more prepared for this event. However, all the preparation in the world will be meaningless if you fail to take action.

---

[5] All of the information listed in this chapter on body language and eye contact has been used with permission from Nightingale-Conant, Inc. from the audio book titled "The Best-Kept Secrets of Great Communicators," by Peter Thomson

Chapter 10
Talking to Your Money Lender

FOR THE UNPREPARED homeowner in a state of mortgage delinquency, speaking with the moneylender's collection agent is a frightening experience. By following my suggestions given in the previous chapters of this book, you will have reduced or completely eliminated most of the unknown factors that would have made you afraid. In most cases the one thing that makes a person afraid is not knowing what is ahead, when you don't know what to expect, what to do and what to say or when you don't know how the other person will react. All these unknowns invite fear and this fear can defeat us before we even the start.

Based on the assumption that you have read the previous chapters of this book and followed my advice to obtain legal counsel, gathered all relevant information concerning the current market conditions and your finances in general, you are more informed than the average homeowner and perhaps even more informed than the bank collection agent. Furthermore, you have worked out an action plan, prepared yourself mentally and emotionally for this juncture, and most importantly, you have prepared a proposal to present to the bank collection agent. Even more, you have considered the responses to the possible objections and rejections that they will throw at your proposal. I can't think of anything else you could possibly do to be any more prepared than you are at this moment. However, failure to take any further action will render all of your previous efforts useless and you will most likely live the rest of your life with the regret of not doing what had to be done. This is not the time to quit; you are very close to the goal. The feat of successfully defending your home from a foreclosure situation is within reach; keep going until you can't go any more, and when you can't go any further, remember the story of the lady that successfully defended her family from a bear attack. That will help motivate you to go at it again until you succeed in defending your home.

I know that even though you are fully prepared for the challenge ahead, there is still a high degree of anxiety and uncertainty within you. It is quite understandable. You are about to call the very same person that has been hounding you day and night, calling you every day and has been sending you threatening letters continuously. The last thing that you want to do is to see that person face-to-face, because his collection tactics sometimes push the limit of what we would consider harassment.

You must find the courage and muster up all of your strength (just like the lady grabbing her frying pan and going after the bear) to take the next step and pick up the phone to make the appointment. Your first tendency will be to delay making the call. You will try to convince yourself that you are not ready for it or that you don't have all the required information or any other excuse that you can come up with. Please remember that the foreclosure clock is ticking and only you have the power to make it stop. The only way to stop the foreclosure procedure is to talk to your lender and work out a new agreement that will be acceptable to both of you.

Please do not procrastinate! Do not delay it, even if you are still missing a few pieces of information. Make the call! Arrange an appointment as soon as you can or arrange a meeting for the following week so that you can gather any needed information that you may be missing. Not only will this give you a few days to find the missing information, but you will also have a few extra days to further prepare yourself. Do not delay the phone call. Time is working against you and the time to take action is now.

Make the appointment

When you call the bank collection agent to set up a personal appointment, he may want to know beforehand the purpose of your visit. He may find it strange that he has been looking for you without success and all of a sudden you are calling him unexpectedly and want to see him in person. Guaranteed, he will want to know what your call is in regards to. After all, he is the one who has been hounding you and threatening you for the last few weeks and now you want to see him face-to-face? I imagine your call will raise some level of apprehension and he will insist on knowing the purpose of your visit.

A word of advice: Avoid giving him too much detail on the purpose of your visit. Simply say that it would be better if you see him in person and in general terms inform him that the purpose of the visit is to discuss a solution to the delay in making your mortgage payments. He will not buy it. I guarantee you that he will want to know more about the purpose of your visit. Simply repeat the same sentence, "It will be better if we discuss this in person." The last thing that you want to do while speaking with him over the phone is to show him your defense plan. The more information you give him while on the phone, the more prepared *he* will be to poke holes in your proposal when you meet. It is in your best interest to give him as little information as possible while on the phone to ensure the highest degree of success in your defense strategy.

Choosing the place and time of the meeting

Selecting the best place for the meeting is quite critical and deserves some consideration, since the bank collection agent does not know how prepared you are for the situation, he will consider that if you are coming to his office, he will have the upper hand. He will feel very uncomfortable outside of his own environment and you want him to feel comfortable so that he can hear every word of your proposal without being distracted by external safety concerns.

Once you reach this point, you must take control of the conversation and you need to lead him to choose a place where *he* feels most comfortable—his own office. What he doesn't know is that you want him to choose that place, and once he selects his own office for the meeting, you don't want the conversation to drag into a long-winded discussion because this is definitely not the best time to start an argument. Stick to your plan; the objective of the call is simply to arrange an appointment. Keep the call as short as possible.

There are two main reasons for doing this. As stated before, the bank collection agent will feel very comfortable and secure in his home environment. It will give him a sense of security, control, and authority. In order to satisfy that need, you will need to give him what he wants. Make him feel as comfortable, secure and in control as possible so that you can get what you want in the end. Another good reason to choose his office as the location for the meeting is that, if you do not like the way the negotiation process is going, you can walk out of the meeting at any time, giving you some reassurance and control.

First, pick the day and time of the appointment. Tell him, "I have Tuesday, Wednesday, and Thursday of next week available. Which day will work best for you?" Once he has chosen a day, tell him, "I am available between 1:00 and 3:30 p.m. Which time works best for you?" Once he chooses a day and time, thank him and tell him that you will see him at the agreed time and date.

Any expert in the human relations field will tell you that you should never schedule an appointment or interview of high importance on a Monday or a Friday; I won't go into detail as to why these are not the best days. Simply keep in mind that the best days of the week to make an appointment are between Tuesday and Thursday, between the hours of 1:00 to 3:30 pm—never on a Monday or on a Friday. However, if those are the only two days of the week that the lending officer is available, and if you have some time left on the foreclosure clock, then you can either reschedule for the following week or accept the appointment on a Monday or a Friday depending on your situation, but insist that the time of the appointment be between 1:00 to 3:30 p.m. If it is at all possible, avoid making the appointment on the first and last day of the workweek.

Can you see what you have done? In the banker's mind, he is now in control of the situation, because you are coming to his environment. He chose the day and time for the meeting, but in reality you led him to the day, time and location of the appointment.

By leading the bank lending officer to do what you had pre-planned for him, your self-confidence will be boosted at the time of the appointment. It will add credibility to your action plan. It will give you some reassurance that by having carefully planned your steps beforehand, you will produce the results that you want.

Explaining your financial situation

The moment of truth has arrived. You are finally going to meet, face-to-face, with the person who has caused you to suffer a great deal of emotional stress over the last few weeks or even months. Before you attend this encounter with the bank collection agent, I encourage you to release any type of anger, resentment, or animosity against this person. Remember, this person is only doing his/her job and if this particular person did not call you, someone else would have done it. Try not to hold that against him.

Furthermore, when you are in his office trying to explain your financial situation, he is still doing his job, and his job is to make you come up with the late payments and to promise that you will never be late again. He will most likely say harsh or even offensive things to you to try to knock you off balance. Keep in mind that these people are trained professionals and they do this every day. They know what buttons to push to get you to respond to their demands and lead you to accept their stipulations.

Regardless of what the banker says or threatens to do to you to intimidate you, keep your cool. Don't allow him to throw you off-center. The best way I know is to pray for him, pray for him before the appointment and during the appointment. Also, forgive him for all the pain and suffering that he has caused you over the last few weeks; really forgive him, and wish for him a successful, healthy life. Speaking from experience, you may have to forgive him *a lot* and many times during this face-to-face encounter.

When you present the banker with your financial situation, you must do it in a clear way and at the same time emphasize the positive aspects of the original mortgage agreement. You may want to highlight that, up until recently, you had been making your regular monthly mortgage payments on time for the last few months, or even years, or whatever the case may be.

You want to tell the bank collection agent the reason you are unable to make your mortgage payments in a single sentence. For example, you may say something like, "I was laid off from my job, due to company downsizing and have not been able to find a suitable job," or "I have been sick in the hospital for the last two months." You will want to show them evidence to verify your claim, like the employment termination letter, or doctor's letter or hospital release letter, etc. You do this for one very good reason; you want to establish credibility. This step will set you apart from all of the other people that have come to talk to him. The great majority of people that come to talk to him bring a long list of excuses; the collection agent has heard them all and they are tired of hearing the same story repeatedly. These homeowners have failed to provide any evidence to prove their claims and are simply seeking sympathy from the bank collection agent.

Furthermore, you will want to tell the banker a little more about your current financial situation to prepare the groundwork for the proposal that you are about to present to him. You will want to show him your income and expense sheet. It will list all your creditors, the minimum monthly payments that you must make to fulfill your other financial obligations as well as your household budget, including the cost of supporting your family.

The income and expense sheet will serve as evidence that explains what the maximum mortgage payment is that you can afford in your current financial situation. This evidence will become very important when you begin to negotiate a lower interest rate on your mortgage or a substantial reduction on your mortgage balance.

In this section, you have accomplished two very important steps. You have established credibility in the eyes of the collection agent by presenting evidence of your claim and secondly you have set the foundation on which all future negotiations will be based.

Presenting the facts

In the previous section, you presented the bank collection agent with the facts concerning your personal financial situation and the reason for which you are unable to make your current mortgage payments. The facts you will be referring to in this section are the facts related to the current real estate market condition in your area, the fair market value of your property, the balance of your mortgage and your late payments.

Before we jump into this topic, I strongly encourage you to purchase a one-inch three-ring-binder with page dividers and tabs where you can label every piece of evidence that you will present to the bank collection agent. In addition, you will want to include a picture of your home and attach it to the front cover of the binder. Make three copies of the binder with all the documents. One copy you will give to the collection agent, you will have another copy with you at the time of the presentation and the third copy you will keep at home as a backup.

Once you finish giving the bank collection agent the overall picture of your financial situation, you need to present the remainder of the facts that you have collected. Start by showing him statistics about the current real estate market in your city or general area.

This document should show the current foreclosure rate in your area, number of properties currently for sale on the market, how many days a property is on the market before it is sold, the difference in asking price and sold price, current mortgage interest rates and real estate market projections over the next three to five years.

The objective in presenting these pieces of evidence to the bank collection agent is to show them that if they insist on taking your house away in a foreclosure proceeding, they will have to absorb a bigger loss in the future. By presenting this evidence in a proper and sequential way for maximum effectiveness, may persuade the collection agent or, at the very least, will lead them to realize that it is in their best interest to work with you to find a solution.

The next piece of evidence that you want to present is the current market evaluation of your property. You will have obtained this information either from an independent real estate appraiser or from a real estate agent. In either case, you need this document to verify the current value of your property. In addition, you may want to include a list of major repairs that may be required on your property, such as a new roof, siding or new carpeting. The objective in presenting this evidence is to show the collection agent the real value of the property. The value of your property may be much lower than the current mortgage balance, based on the current market condition. Secondly, if the bank is unwavering in their decision to take away your home, they will have to absorb a bigger loss, especially if there are expensive repairs that must be done to the house prior to being offered for sale on the open market.

Once the bank takes possession of your home, they will want to recover their losses in the shortest amount of time. In order for the bank to recover their losses quickly, they will be forced to lower the asking price and hope for a quick sale. However, you will have already proven to them that the current real value of your home is lower than the mortgage balance. Consider it from the consumer's point of view. What would motivate you to purchase a house for more than the current value, especially if you would incur additional expensive repairs, when you could go down the street and buy something better that does not require repairs for a lower price? Once you present this piece of evidence to the bank, it will become absolutely clear to them that it is in their best interest to work with you.

The last piece of information that you will present to them is your current mortgage balance, which includes the late mortgage payments and fees. They already have this information and they know exactly how much you owe them.

By presenting them with their own mortgage balance information right after you have shown them the current market value of your property, you will have defeated them on their own territory with their own information. How can they continue to insist on demanding payment from you, when they have lost the moral ground to do it? Legally speaking they can still demand payment, but morally speaking they can't. You have successfully disarmed them and if it was not clear before, they have no other choice but to negotiate an alternate agreement with you, by either forgiving a portion of your mortgage balance to bring it to par with the market or by lowering the mortgage interest rate or a combination of both.

Solicit help from your lender

Now that you have made your point very clear to the collection agent, there should be no arguing against the evidence. The evidence speaks for itself. Now you can proceed to solicit their assistance in a very gentle and polite way.

This idea is brilliant, you have successfully disarmed the banker with the evidence that you brought along, and furthermore, you have taken the time to emotionally involve him by presenting him your income and expense sheet. You may want to say something like, "If you were me, what would you do in this situation?" I would be very surprised if, after presenting him with all these irrefutable facts, he responds by saying something like, "*I would make up the mortgage payments and learn to live with it.*" Most likely, he will not know what to say. You may want to repeat the question in a different way. What would you do if your mortgage balance was higher than the fair market value of your property and you barely had enough money to feed your family? By phrasing the question in such a way, you are getting the banker personally involved and touching his emotions.

After you ask him the question for the second time, stay quiet for a while. By remaining quiet, you are allowing him to mentally and emotionally involve himself in your situation and he will be more open to consider alternative ways to help you. Logically, he will reason that by helping you, he is helping himself and his employer.

Do not interrupt him while he is thinking about your situation; allow him enough time to get emotionally involved. I can't tell you a specific length of time to give him, but by watching him, you will know when he is done thinking. I have no way of knowing what his response will be. You need to give him the time to verbalize his thoughts and carefully listen to what he has to say. Who knows, he may propose to make all the concessions that you have asked of him. Once you have made your situation personal to the banker, you may want to ask him another question to raise your situation to the next level. You may want to say something like this: "*I would imagine that over the last few years your bank has had to deal with a number of these types of situations. Is your bank offering any type of alternative financing programs for homeowners in these circumstances?"*

By now, the banks have learned the costly lesson of taking home-owners through the foreclosure process. They have also learned that it is not in their best interest to continue in that direction. They would much rather take an alternate route to deal with delinquent homeowners and many banks have created alternate programs, that sometimes are financed by the government, to help homeowners in danger of losing their home.

You really want to pay attention to what the bank has to offer. It may be something much better than what you are about to propose. Another rule of negotiation is: *"In a negotiation, he who speaks first loses."* Therefore, you want the bank to be the first one to speak after you have presented all your evidence.

Propose a solution to your lender

Do not be surprised if, after presenting your case with all the irrefu-table evidence regarding your financial situation and the current mar-ket condition, the collection agent continues to demand full payment from you. It is a defense mechanism. The agent is fully aware that he has been defeated with his own information, but he is unwilling to admit defeat. He will resort back to his training and may raise his voice and threaten you, even though he has lost the moral ground to make such demands.

Stay calm. Simply look at him and allow him to entangle himself in his own words. He may say offensive or hurtful words to you in or-der to upset you and knock you off balance.

As he goes on and on with his rant, keep calm. Remember that when someone gets angry, he is simply expressing how afraid he really is. Pray for him and forgive him for all of the insulting words he is throwing at you. Do not allow his poor attitude to contaminate yours. Remember that you have come to this meeting with a purpose and your mission has not yet been accomplished. You are very close to reaching your goal, now is not the time to start an argument with the collection agent. Keep quiet, you will win this round by keeping silent. Do not respond to insults and aggressive behavior, stay calm. Eventually he will run out of things to say and will realize that he has been defeated.

If he continues to go on and on, you have two choices. One is that you stand up and tell him/her in a firm, stern voice that you will call back to make another appointment once his/her state of mind has improved and walk out of his office. The other is to be bold and take control of the situation by instructing him to be quiet and listen so that you can present him with a proposal that will be beneficial to both the bank and to you. He may really appreciate your bold move as he may be getting tired of arguing with himself.

This may be one of many ways of presenting your proposal to the collection agent, and I am in no way suggesting that this is the best and only way. I strongly suggest that you come up with your own approach to present your case. However, you may say something like this: "I have studied my financial situation and the current real estate market condition. I also know that it is not in the bank's best interest to foreclose on my property. I also don't want to lose my home in a foreclosure. Could we work out an arrangement in a way that it could be a win situation for both of us? What I propose is this …" and you list all the concessions that the bank needs to make in order for you to be able to meet your financial obligations. At the same time you must reassure the banker that by his agreeing to your concessions you will be making your monthly payments without fail every month.

Reassuring the bank of your commitment to faithfully make the mortgage payments will greatly improve your chances of obtaining a positive outcome to this situation.

What if the bank says NO?

Is there a possibility that the bank would refuse to help you, even with all the irrefutable evidence that you have presented to them, showing that it is in its best interest to help you? Yes, there is a possibility that the banker may simply say no, and there could be a number of good reasons why he could refuse to work with you.

One perfectly good reason is that the bank does not have the funds to forgive a large percentage of your mortgage balance. The bank may be teetering on going under. Although, this is a good reason, it is highly unlikely that it will go under due to government intervention in the financial market. Another reason may be that the bank collection agent dislikes delinquent homeowners and they simply have a corporate policy not to negotiate with this type of homeowner. This is an unwritten rule in the banking industry, especially when you are negotiating a short sale on the property (short sale is a commonly known term. It refers to negotiating a reduction in the principal balance of the mortgage). The bank will refuse to budge. The representative will refuse to give the struggling homeowner a reduction in his mortgage balance even if the bank loses many more thousands of dollars in the process. However, if I come as an investor and offer the bank ten cents on the dollar, it will accept the offer. Please, don't ask me why banks do that; I just know that they do it quite often.

They do not like to negotiate a reduction on the mortgage balance to delinquent homeowners, but are willing to do so for an investor.

Another reason could be that this particular bank or credit union has a mandate or a policy established by the board of directors that states that it will not, under any circumstances, negotiate or lower the mortgage balance on any of its mortgages. We are beginning to see this more often in smaller banks and credit unions. Struggling banks can't cope with the massive losses they have endured over the last few years. What these banks have found is that there is a great need for rental units (the same information that I gave you earlier in the book). Therefore, over the past few months, once they acquire a property through foreclosure, instead of offering the property on the open market where they will have to take a bigger loss, they are now hiring a real estate managing company to rent the property. By renting the property out, the bank will have steady income from delinquent properties, which is what they wanted in the first place. All that the bank wants is to have someone make the mortgage payments and in many cases, they are able to rent the properties for much more than the original monthly mortgage amount. Furthermore, banks are now able to remove that property from their list of NPA (non-performing assets) and the benefits do not stop there. They save themselves thousands of dollars in realtor fees, holding fees and maintenance fees. They can also now afford to sit on that property until the real estate market turns around, and then they may be able to sell that property at a profit.

As banks became more and more desperate to generate income, they were forced to adjust to the market condition and become creative in order to survive this financial crisis. Banks are currently taking the approach: "The best way to make money is to stop losing money." That is exactly what they have done. Once they have possession of the property, it is turned into a rental property. Currently we are seeing this type of adjustment with the smaller banks; it is still in the 'test phase.' However, I anticipate that other banks will follow suit if they see the smaller banks turning a profit with this new system.

Alternative options

If your current bank is unwilling or unable to help you, what can you do? It all depends on where you are in the foreclosure process, how much time you have available and which of the three conditions your property is in.

If you are ahead or breaking even with the value of your property, you could simply attempt to get a new mortgage from a different banking institution. Most mortgages are approved in less than two weeks and if time is getting too tight and you have to make a court appearance, you could ask the court for an extension. For the most part, the judge will grant you the request as long as you can prove that you are doing something to resolve the foreclosure demand. I am fully aware that the new bank may have some apprehension in giving you a new mortgage but you can help reassure the banker by getting a co-signer on the new mortgage.

The situation becomes more difficult if you are in an underwater situation. In this case, your options are very limited and as mentioned in the previous chapters, if the bank is unwilling to work with you, you only have two choices. One is to allow the bank to take your property away, but we want to avoid that option, because of the undesirable consequences that you would have to bear for the next few years. In this case the other viable alternative would be to do exactly the same thing that the bank is doing: Either rent out the property to someone else for more money than your mortgage payment or create a lease-to-own rental agreement.

If you rent your property out to someone else, assuming that the bank is not willing to budge an inch, you will have to make up late payments and fees, but you may not have the money to do that. Furthermore, if you rent out your property, you would need to live somewhere else. If you do not have relatives or friends that can give you temporary shelter for a few months, you most likely do not have the money for a security deposit and the first month's rent. If this is the case, your only other option would be to create a lease-to-own rental agreement[6].

The advantage of a lease-to-own rental agreement is that you will have someone to make the mortgage payments for you. At the same time you will have collected at least a five percent down payment on your property. This money will enable you to make up the late mortgage payments and fees, and you will have more than enough money to pay for the security deposit and the first month's rent on the rental unit. You may even have a few thousand dollars left to help you out for a few months until you are able to secure a job or another source income.

Regardless of the outcome, you will have done your best to defend your home. You will live your life without regret. If you are successful, and I sincerely hope that you are successful in defending the roof over your head, I congratulate you and I rejoice that I was able to help at least one person by sharing my own experience. If you are not successful, I am sorry that I was not much help to you. However, remember the six words that my wife used to say to me: "*Everything is going to be o.k.*" I am a living testimony of those six words.

---

[6] Refer to Chapter 6 and Appendix C.

Looking back and pondering that particular situation in my life, my wife was right and I can tell you now that everything turned out okay. In fact, losing our house in a foreclosure was the best thing that could have happened to us. Once I was released from the burden of carrying a mortgage payment that I could not afford, it presented me with the opportunity to finish my education. My education allowed me to build a successful carrier and even now, it has allowed me to share my story with you, to give you hope and encouragement that in the course of time, *"Everything is going to be o.k."*

I wish you the best in your endeavor to defend your home and I pray that the Lord will give you the strength and courage to accept His will in your situation.

APPENDIX A

Part A—To evaluate the comparable homes in your area, complete the following:

House Sale Comparables

*Please refer to Chapter 3 for more information or visit www.thefaraciousmphenomenon.com

CALGARY WEALTH PARTNERS
*This information was obtained and used courtesy of Calgary Wealth Partners

Address	Bedrooms	Baths	Square Footage	Sold Price	Sales Date	Year Built
1305 2nd Avenue	3	2	2,005	$225,000	May-14	2001
1.						
2.						
3.						
4.						
5.						
6.						
7.						
8.						
9.						
10.						

* To obtain a list of comparables in your area speak to a real estate agent. Ask your real estate agent/broker to provide you a list of comparable homes similar to your home in square footage, style and upgrades. Ask for the **sold comparables**, not the listed comparables in your area over the last 6 month to a year.

Part B—In order to obtain the "Average Sold Price per Square Foot" in your area, complete the following:

CALGARY WEALTH PARTNERS
*This information was obtained and used courtesy of Calgary Wealth Partners

Market Value Comparables			
*Please refer to Chapter 3 for more information or visit www.theforeclosurephenomenon.com			
Address	**Sold Price**	**Square Footage**	**Cost Per Square Footage**
1305 2nd Avenue	$225,000	2,005	$112.22
1.			
2.			
3.			
4.			
5.			
6.			
7.			
8.			
9.			
10.			
		Average Cost Per Square Foot	
		Market Value = Average Cost Per Square Foot * Your Property's square footage	

Step 1: To calculate the "Cost per Square Footage," input the numbers obtained from the "House Sale Comparables" (Part A) spreadsheet into "Market Value Comparables" (Part B) spreadsheet.

Step 2: To calculate the "Cost per Square Footage," divide the "Sold Price" by the "Square Footage" of that house.

Step 3: Discard the highest and lowest "Cost per Square Footage" numbers and only work with the numbers in between.

Step 4: Add the remaining "Cost per Square Footage" numbers together.

Step 5: Divide that number by the number of comparable houses you used (Ex: If you used 6 houses, divide the "Cost per Square Footage" value by 6). This will give you the "AVERAGE Cost per Square Foot" in your area.

Step 6: To obtain the "Market Value" of your home, multiply the "Average Cost per Square Foot" by the square footage of *your* house.

* When presenting this information to the bank collection agent, ensure you also include a list of repairs needed for your house and the cost of each repair.

If you would like a free downloadable version of this spreadsheet, please visit http://www.theforeclosurephenomenon.com

APPENDIX B

Below is a sample spreadsheet you can use to create a household budget for yourself and to demonstrate your financial situation to your collection agent. A free downloadable copy is available at

http://www.theforeclosurephenomenon.com

CALGARY WEALTH PARTNERS
*This information was obtained and used courtesy of Calgary Wealth Partners

Monthly Household Budget	
Date:	
Income	
Net Income (or self-employment earnings)	
Spouse's Net Income	
Rental Income	
Pension Income	
Employment Insurance/ Worker's Comp.	
*Other income (ex/ public Assistance, alimony etc.)	
*Other income (ex/ public Assistance, alimony etc.)	
Total Income	$0.00
Fixed Monthly Expenses	
Mortgage Payments	
Property Tax/Condo fees (1/12 of annual total)	
*Other Loans (ex/ line of credit, second mortgage etc.)	
Car/Lease Payment(s)	
Car Insurance	
Homeowners Insurance	
Life Insurance	
Utilities (gas, water, heating)	
Alimony/Child Support/Childcare	
Medical/Healthcare	
Credit card/Department store (min. payment)	
Credit card/Department store (min. payment)	
Credit card/Department store (min. payment)	
Total Fixed Monthly Expenses	$0.00
Variable Monthly Expenses	
Groceries	
Clothing	
Car Repairs/Maintenance (including license renewal)	
Travel (gasoline/parking/toll fees)	
Other Travel Expenses (transit pass/ taxi etc.)	
Telephone/Cellphone	
Cable/Satellite/Internet	
House Maintenance	
Book, Subscriptions	
Personal Care/Toiletries	
Charitable Donations (ex/ church)	
Laundry/Dry Cleaning	
Tuition fees	
Entertainment (ex/ dining, movies, coffee etc.)	
Gifts	
Miscellaneous (ex/ pet care)	
Cigarettes/Alcohol	
*Other	
Total Variable Expenses	$0.00
Total Income	$0.00
Total Expenses (Add Total Fixed + Variable Expenses)	$0.00
Net Income (Subtract Total Income - Total Expenses)	**$0.00**

APPENDIX C

"Peter Thomson is one of the UK's leading strategists in the areas of communication and personal and business growth. He has a very diverse history and, along with his other ventures, has been a very successful entrepreneur. Having started in business in 1972, he built and sold three successful companies, enabling him to retire at age 42. Far from living the leisurely life, however, Peter is an active public speaker, motivator, and writer, having published three books, six tips booklets, and over a dozen audio programs with Nightingale-Conant. One of his most recent accomplishments has been an Honorary Doctorate (Doctor of Letters) from The American Intercontinental University for his work in communication skills and helping others to succeed in life."

To obtain the link to the full version of Peter Thompson's program titled, *"The Best Kept Secrets of Great Communicators"* through Nightingale-Conant please visit:

http://www.theforeclosurephenomenon.com

APPENDIX D

Lease-to-own agreements vary from state to state and from province to province. It is nearly impossible to create one universal form for this purpose. I suggest you obtain a standard rental agreement in your specific state/province and include the items in the list found below.

I strongly encourage you to speak to an attorney or a real estate agent who is well versed in lease-to-own agreements in order to complete a lease-to-own agreement that will adhere to your specific state/province laws and regulations.

Lease-to-Own Agreement Guidelines

1. The length of the lease (Typically 6 months to 2 years).
2. The monthly rent amount.
3. The end date for the lease and any late fees that may be imposed.
4. A description of the security deposit.
5. Whether or not the security deposit is refundable.
6. Conditions of how the deposit may be refunded.
7. Who is responsible for the repairs/maintenance and to what amount (Typically under $500).
8. Require the tenant to maintain renters insurance.
9. Terms of renewal (if offered).
10. The purchase price of home and the specific way the purchase price was determined.
11. How options considerations and credits will work.
12. How the tenant/buyer qualifies for those credits.
13. Who will hold the credits (ex/ escrow).
14. Who has access to the credits and under what circumstances.
15. How refunds will be handled, if you allow them.
16. A statement stating that the title will not be transferred to the buyer until after closing.
17. Specify that this is a lease-to-own agreement not a mortgage agreement.

About the Author

A native of El Salvador, Joaquin came to North America at the impressionable age of sixteen in the early eighties. He has spent most of his adult life in the province of Alberta, Canada where he currently lives with his wife, children and grandchildren.

In his first 15 years after arriving in North America, Joaquin had to overcome the many challenges that every immigrant experiences. Some of those challenges included learning a new language, overcoming culture barriers and having a lack of formal education, all while raising his three young daughters. It was also during this time he experienced great financial stress. Joaquin learned many valuable lessons, which he is now willing and able to share with the rest of the world through this book.

Joaquin highly regards education and even though he only has a diploma in Civil Engineering at this time, he encourages everyone to acquire the highest level of education possible. The education that he obtained taught him how to use his mind to think creatively, enabling him to come up with unique solutions to challenging problems. However, he credits all the success in his life in finding Jesus Christ as his savior.

CPSIA information can be obtained at www.ICGtesting.com
Printed in the USA
LVOW132316280313

326559LV00001B/51/P